Ambivalent Journey

Richard C. Jones

AMBIVALENT JOURNEY

U.S. Migration
and Economic Mobility in
North-Central Mexico

The University of Arizona Press   *Tucson and London*

The University of Arizona Press
Copyright © 1995
Arizona Board of Regents
All rights reserved

00 99 98 97 96 6 5 4 3 2 1

Library of Congress Cataloging-in-Publication Data

Jones, Richard C., 1942–
    Ambivalent journey : U.S. migration and economic mobility in north-central Mexico / Richard C. Jones.
          p.   cm.
    Includes bibliographical references and index.
    ISBN 0-8165-1473-9 (alk. paper)
    1. Zacatecas (Mexico : State)—Emigration and immigration.
2. Coahuila (Mexico : State)—Emigration and immigration.   3. United
States—Emigration and immigration.   4. Zacatecas (Mexico : State)—
Economic conditions.   5. Coahuila (Mexico : State)—Economic
conditions.   6. Immigrants—United States.   7. Mexicans—United
States.   8. Alien labor—United States.   I. Title.
JV7401.J66   1995   94-18754
304.8'73072'14—dc20   CIP

British Library Cataloguing-in-Publication Data
A catalogue record for this book is available
from the British Library.

Contents

Figures

Tables

Preface

The writing of this book has been an excursion into how migration to the United States affects the livelihoods of families in two subregions of north-central Mexico. It has also been a quest to sort through the antithetical arguments and the ambiguous terminology with which the literature bristles, in order to come up with concepts that clarify rather than confuse. More broadly and personally, this book has offered me the opportunity to look deep into rural Mexico, where buried in the canyons and foothills and on the rivers and plateaus of the Sierra Madres are villages which are effectively laborsheds for secondary labor-market jobs in large cities all across the southwestern United States. These places, so quintessentially Mexican, are intimately tied with the United States. Their fathers, sons, uncles, and brothers have come to depend upon the United States for sustenance, even though their hearts are left behind in their homelands. We have come to depend on these migrants, too, but our dependency is ignored, hidden because of their usually clandestine status. The U.S.-Mexican border has been called a sieve, but it is also a mirror—a huge one-way mirror that is transparent northward but opaque southward. To the south, migrants in the smallest towns know a great deal about life and opportunities in Los Angeles, San Diego, Dallas, and San Antonio. Yet the average resident of those cities knows practically nothing about life a few hundred miles to the south. I will have fulfilled my purpose if I have revealed to my audience something about the lives, hopes, and tribulations of this shadow population who harvest our vegetables, build our homes, serve our meals, sew our clothing, landscape our lawns, and care for our children.

I would like to acknowledge the National Science Foundation for the grant (#SES-8619504) which made this book possible. I also thank my student research assistants, Michael Perez, from the United States, and Maria Maya, Lourdes Orta, Beatriz Ramírez, Amilcar Saavedra, Ricardo de León,

Myriam Durán, Lourdes Guzman, and Norma Saucedo, from Mexico. I appreciate their patiently enduring the mini-crises that inevitably accompany taking a binational team of urbanites, both men and women, into the recesses of backroads Mexico for weeks at a time, with nothing to do in their spare time but try to solve little puzzles brought along by their professor. The students' mentoring professors, Anne Reid of the Autonomous Metropolitan University in Mexico City and Breen Murray of the University of Monterrey, did me an invaluable service in recruiting them, even suffering (almost) silently the indignity of learning that I had originally planned to pay the students more than their own university salaries.

In Mexico it seems that in any small town there are dozens of people in government, in business, and in the professions who are willing to take a group of fledgling student interviewers and their professor under their wings and help them not only with data and contacts, but to get to know the community and its attractions. This helpfulness was also characteristic of our interviewees, many of whom later became friends. I want all these people to know how uplifting and enabling their hospitality has been, and that the summary reports I promised them really are forthcoming.

At the University of Texas at San Antonio, my colleagues Tom Baylis, David Kowalewski, and Avelardo Valdez provided critical comments on my original research proposal, which I appreciate. I also thank Richard Harris and Avelardo Valdez, coauthors with me of early (pioneering, I would say) studies of occupational mobility of migrants from Dolores Hidalgo, Guanajuato, and of spatial mobility of Hispanics and undocumenteds in San Antonio. Working with them gave me many new ideas. My division director in Social and Policy Sciences, David Alvírez, has been helpful and encouraging during the past five years during which this research has been analyzed, written up, and revised. His help has taken many forms, from giving me extra copying funds to codirecting a field course and research project on migration and social change in Cedral, San Luis Potosí, the preliminary results from which have provided me insights that have become a part of this book.

At the University of Arizona Press, editor Christine Szuter was consistently enthusiastic about the book's prospects. I also thank two anonymous outside reviewers for their time and encouragement. I am especially indebted to my talented copyeditor, Suzanne Schafer, who unfailingly comprehended my meaning in obscure passages and elucidated them with skill and insight.

My mother, a high school Spanish teacher, stimulated my childhood interest in Mexico and gave me the combination of compassion and curiosity which have so helped my academic career. My father instilled in me the complementary qualities of critical judgment and perseverance. All of these qualities have served me well in the writing of this book.

My son Rick and my daughter Katrina have been an inexhaustible pool of respite from the tediousness of this project. They had to do totally without me for six months while I was in the field and then, to add insult to injury, to do without my full attention for almost six years while the book was being completed. Despite my long absences, I could not have done it without them.

There is no one I owe more to than my wife, Maria Maya Jones. Her contributions are everywhere in the book. It was she who set the example for the original interview team in Zacatecas, and again for the team in Coahuila, with her uncanny ability to empathize with her interviewees and win their confidence. She did follow-up interviews with me in Zacatecas on several occasions. She coded and computerized most of the household and establishment data. She gave me her opinions on countless questions that arose during the writing of the book. She gave me a new reason to complete the book—our son Christopher. His natural love of things both Mexicano and Norteamericano reflects my own love of both cultures. I hope that this is evident in the book.

Ambivalent Journey

The phenomenon of seasonal U.S. migration tends to perpetuate itself—a process I refer to as the migrant syndrome *—an ever-growing dependency on foreign wage labor. . . . Out-migration has actually undermined the development of the town's agricultural economy . . . [by] leaving even fewer residents behind to cultivate local fields, [and converting] prime agricultural lands into seasonal pasture. (Reichert 1981, 62–64)*

Given the experience of labor migration in many households and communities, venturing forth in search of additional income does not entail heavy risk of failure, especially by comparison with the probable results of remaining in the local community. . . . Labor migration is a means to maintain rural roots, not to leave them. . . . Many households carry on as before, . . . [substituting] hired labor for migrating family labor, . . . [shifting to] less labor-intensive crops and using more female and child labor. (Grindle 1988, 38).

1

Introduction
The Research Record

These two quotations, the first by an anthropologist and the second by a rural development specialist, exemplify the diversity of views on the impacts of U.S. migration on communities of origin in rural west-central Mexico. (Throughout this book, the term *U.S. migration* refers to migration to and from the United States to work.) The first sees dependency and disinvestment; the second sees greater household autonomy and the maintenance of rural livelihoods. Both writers would agree that U.S. migration does not lead to local economic development. Yet even this view may be questioned, given recent innovative joint ventures among migrants, government, and private agribusiness in states such as Zacatecas (Jones and Maya 1991).

Similar diversity can be found in the experiences of migrants themselves. One remarkable conclusion from the many "village" studies is that adjacent Mexican towns and *municipios* (counties) may have very different U.S. migration experiences. For example, here are two migrant vignettes, from interviews by the author in early 1988 with families from adjacent municipios in central Zacatecas:

José Luis Ortega is a 53-year-old farmer from Tayahua, a small town in Villanueva municipio, central Zacatecas (and, incidentally, the hometown of the famous Mexican singer and actor Antonio Aguilar). José worked first as a *bracero* (contractual farmworker in the United States) in 1960. Since then, he, his wife, and their nine children have made some twenty trips (totaling over twenty years) to factory jobs in the north, chiefly in Illinois. Migration has become a way of life for them, and five children now live in Illinois, with legal papers. José, his wife, and the other four children live in Mexico; when they return to the United States, they do so as *mojados* (illegals, or "wetbacks"). In 1987, the $800 they received from work in the

United States paid three-fourths of their family expenses—food, clothing, school expenses, and home improvements—yet the family remains quite poor. They practice a little agriculture, growing corn and beans. But basically, like many of the families of Tayahua, they are waiting for the right conditions to return to work and join family members in the United States. They have lost many of their ties with their town and with Mexico, and feel like strangers in their homeland.

Manuel Viramontes is a 55-year-old farmer from Cargadero, a village in Jerez municipio, which is adjacent to Villanueva municipio in central Zacatecas. He worked as a bracero at different points during 1945–65. During 1970–85, he and six of his children worked as mojados picking and packing fruit in California. During that time, they returned every year or two to Mexico to work and live. In 1972, Manuel invested his U.S. earnings to begin a peach orchard in Cargadero, based on skills he learned picking peaches south of San Francisco. Like many of his neighbors, he continued to invest his U.S. earnings in the orchard. He and his wife now live almost entirely on his Mexican earnings—some $10,000 per year—and he has not found it necessary to return to the United States since 1985. He is proud to be able to "stay at home with [his] little trees."

These vignettes do not necessarily represent the typical migrant families of their respective municipios. On the other hand, they do represent two important subtypes. The Ortegas illustrate dependency and disinvestment; the Viramontes, autonomy and reinvestment. Which subtype predominates is one of the critical questions addressed in this book. The answer is found in the results of a survey questionnaire administered during the first six months of 1988 to over one thousand families in two subregions known for their high U.S. migration rates—central Zacatecas and northern Coahuila.

Kritz, Keely, and Tomasi (1981) identify three major themes in the literature on international migration: international relations, economic development, and migrant integration into host societies. Clearly, development is the critical concern of the literature on impacts of emigration on local sending areas. Because the goal of this book is to clarify and elaborate on that literature, my approach is economic rather than political (as might be implied in the first theme) or cultural (as implied by the third theme). The book draws heavily from economic and population geography, regional economics, and demography. However, the concepts I present will be explained in a way that should be understandable to the educated reader.

Despite the many international migration studies that have been carried out, no one can seem to agree on whether the impacts of migration on areas of origin are principally positive or negative. In part this is because researchers use different units of analysis (individual, family, state, region, etc.), study different parts of the world, and come from different disciplines (anthropology, political science, sociology, economics). In addition, some studies have considered migration as an invariant state as opposed to an evolving process. The rest of this chapter discusses the international literature on origin impacts of wage-labor migration—that is, its effects upon the families, villages, and regions from which the migrants come. The conclusions from the Mexican village studies are then investigated in light of this literature. Finally, a more comprehensive theory is offered that helps to explain some of the different conclusions encountered in the literature.

Chapter 2 gives an overview of the two subregions investigated in this book: central Zacatecas and northern Coahuila. It provides an important explanatory context for the chapters which follow, because independent of the factors differentiating one family's level of migration from another's there are underlying factors that explain why the entire region sends migrants to the United States. These factors include the local physical geography, history, economy, and political climate.

Chapter 3 compares the levels of U.S. migration across historical periods and between subregions and municipios. Then it explains differences in household migration in terms of demographic characteristics such as the age, education, and occupation of the household head and the size of the family. In so doing, it describes migration selectivity; that is, it tells us who goes and who stays in each subregion.

Chapter 4, "U.S. Migration and Household Economic Behavior," is the heart of the book. It seeks answers to the many questions that the literature on village studies has left open. Do migrant households spend their new earnings chiefly on consumer goods, or do they invest them in the family's social welfare and in productive enterprises? Do migrant households spend and invest most of their money outside the local community? Does migration make rich families richer, or does it allow poor families to catch up? Is the impact of migration on the family in central Zacatecas, a poor mining and grazing area of central Mexico, significantly different from its impact in northern Coahuila, a dynamic industrial and agribusiness area close to the U.S. border?

Chapter 5 chronicles the life histories of actual heads of household in Zacatecas and Coahuila. These persons were selected from among those who completed survey questionnaires and reinterviewed in depth about both the reasons for and the effects of their migration to the United States. They represent different positions along the continuum from long-term, active migrant to nonmigrant. Their experiences illustrate many of the generalizations in chapters 3 and 4.

Chapter 6 shifts the focus from the family to the community. It compares the study communities in Zacatecas with respect to their economic gains from U.S. migration, and examines whether these gains generate more local growth than do those from other external-income-generating (basic) activities including internal migration, commuting, commercial agriculture, and other private business activities. The trilateral approval of the North American Free Trade Agreement (NAFTA) has generated considerable optimism that new, export-oriented employment will stem illegal movement into the United States originating in the migration hearth of central Mexico. In chapter 6 we examine whether this optimism is well founded or not. Zacatecas alone is examined, because the relatively small number of study communities in Coahuila makes comparison across communities too problematical.

The final chapter recapitulates the book's principal conclusions and elaborates on the scenario in which free trade–generated employment might supplant U.S. migration as a basic income source for central Zacatecas.

International Labor Migration and the Area of Origin
Spatial Patterns on the Global Scale

The migration stream from Mexico to the United States is one of some two dozen major streams of wage-labor migrants in the world. Following Keely and Tran (1989), I will use "unrequited transfers" of money into a country (which essentially consist of the remittances flowing into that country from its nationals overseas) as a measure of the importance of wage-labor migration to the country. I will arbitrarily consider $100 million (U.S.) of unrequited transfers in 1985 as the amount that separates the major from the minor remittance-receiving countries (Keely and Tran 1989). By this criterion, in 1985 twenty-three countries were major recipients of remittances, and they accounted for 97 percent of the total positive unrequited transfers in the world. The major remittance-

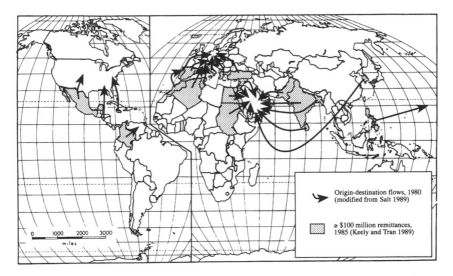

Figure 1.1 Major international wage-labor flows

receiving countries are predominantly subtropical and temperate lands of Middle America, the Mediterranean, and South Asia (fig. 1.1). Among the twenty-three, some (such as Mexico and Algeria) are middle-income developing countries, others (such as India and the Sudan) are low-income developing countries, and still others (such as Spain and Greece) are developed countries of the European periphery. Thus, countries all along the development spectrum are involved in wage-labor migration.

The remittances which support these countries originate in three major world regions—the Persian Gulf, northwestern Europe, and the United States. (The origin-destination arrows in figure 1.1 are after Keely and Tran 1989, Salt 1989, and other sources.) The Persian Gulf dominates the world pattern; in fact, remittances from and migration into the region have increased dramatically since 1960, recently involving countries farther afield in South and East Asia. The remittance flows from Europe, interestingly, continue to be strong despite the fact that actual migration into Europe has been sharply curtailed since 1972 by countries such as Germany (Hoskin and Fitzgerald 1989), the United Kingdom (Layton-Henry 1989), and France. This is the case because previously settled migrants continue to remit to their home countries. Migration into and remittances from the United States also continue at high levels, having grown since 1960 at rates somewhere between those for the Persian Gulf and those for Europe. Only one migration stream—that from Colombia to Venezuela—is destined elsewhere than these three world regions.

In the Western Hemisphere, Mexico's remittance receipts are closely challenged by those of Colombia for the top position. However, even when we account for substantial undocumented migrant remittances, neither of these Western countries' receipts rival those of countries like Portugal, Egypt, Turkey, India, or Pakistan. Among the twenty-three top countries in wage-labor remittances, Mexico is somewhere near the middle.

A quick perusal of the literature with this world pattern in mind reveals that case studies of origin-area impacts have indeed covered many of these twenty-three countries. In the Western Hemisphere, for example, a great deal has been written about the impacts of remittances on Mexico, the Caribbean, and Colombia; in the Eastern Hemisphere, articles have been written about their impacts on Jordan, India, Pakistan, the Philippines, Spain, Portugal, Italy, Turkey, Greece, and other countries. However, the effects of remittances on the countries of Central America, North Africa, and parts of the Middle East have been neglected in the literature. This should be taken into account when reading the following generalizations.

The Structural Perspective

"Structuralists," including those who take a political economy or dependency approach and have been influenced by writers such as Frank (1981), Gonzalez-Casanova (1965), and Dos Santos (1973), examine migration's impact upon a sending society's autonomy and equality and on the maintenance of its social institutions. Citing evidence that migrants are dependent on events completely outside of their control, noting that migration benefits some groups over others, and observing that migrant-sending societies are vulnerable to cultural changes injected from host societies, the structuralists generally take a negative view of international migration. The structural perspective on international migration was most pronounced in the period before 1982. Authors espousing this perspective tended to study specific villages or to summarize research at the village scale. (Impact studies dealing specifically with Mexico are discussed separately in the next section.)

World systems theory, originally espoused by Wallerstein (1979, 1980), is one of the most recent expressions of the structuralist argument. International migration is addressed only obliquely by this theory, which deals primarily with international trade and investment. The theory suggests that the importation of low-wage labor from peripheral countries (such as Mexico) is a mechanism by which declining hegemonic powers (such as the United States) preserve the profitability of their industries in the face of increasing costs and international competition (de Oliver 1993). Trade liberalization (e.g., NAFTA) may, however, in time provide the hegemonic power with a superior method for increasing profitability, that is, by locating its industries abroad, thereby accessing cheap labor directly without having to pay the social costs of an immigrant labor force. In fact, restrictions on immigrant labor may be imposed by the hegemon (as in the recent stiffening of U.S. immigration policy, particularly toward undocumented migrants from Mexico).

Principal among the negative consequences identified by the structuralists is increased dependency on a less stable, external source of income. Control of the local economy shifts from local factors, over which families have some control, to international forces over which they have no control. The sending society cannot catch up economically with the host society, owing to the host society's continued comparative advantages in the production of capital goods and services (Portes 1978). Therefore, the wage differential between the societies persists and even widens. Families send migrants again and again—the migrant syndrome—but the sending society does not develop (Shrestha 1985).

Another negative impact is disinvestment in the local economy, including the abandonment of traditional livelihoods. Remittances are likely to be spent on an improved standard of living rather than on development capital—especially since remittances come "not in mighty rivers, but in drips and drops" (Swanson 1979). In marginal agricultural areas, migrants do not purchase agricultural inputs for improving productivity, but instead buy land for resale or eventual retirement (Brana-Shute and Brana-Shute 1982; Fergany 1982; Rhoades 1979).

Furthermore, according to this theory, the transfer of skills between host and origin countries is minimal, and there is out-migration of labor and skills that are needed locally. Agricultural workers abroad, for example, learn few skills which are applicable to the products in demand at home. Moreover, attitudes change such that after earning high salaries abroad, the return migrant tends to depreciate all forms of local work (Piore 1979, 115–40). Loss of professionals (e.g., teachers) trained in the country may occur through migration (Shah 1983). Many migrants return home not to innovate and invest but to relax or retire (Bohning 1975).

Still another negative impact is the increase in social and economic in-equalities within the sending area. Over time, a migrant elite develops whose superior housing, land ownership, and household possessions set them apart from nonmigrants. Also, since the members of this elite do little work while at home, envy and resentment develop among the other villa-gers (McArthur 1979; Griffiths 1979).

Finally, social disintegration occurs both within the family and within the village. With the adoption of host-country values that migration brings, there is less acceptance of parental authority, less support of the extended family and of the social institutions such as the church (or temple or mosque), and more exasperation with local politics. With the ability of migrants to earn high incomes overseas without much education, the value of local schooling is depreciated. With the male head of household absent for long periods, children are undisciplined and may suffer from a variety of psychological stresses. The extended family is split, and the household adopts a self-centered approach to economic and social mobility (Cobbe 1982; Eikaas 1979).

The Functional Perspective

Functionalists, influenced by the work of Rostow (1960), Hirschman (1958), and Friedmann (1966), among others, emphasize the effects of migration on economic growth and modernization both at the family level and at the regional level. Citing evidence that many families and individuals benefit economically, that remittances are invested in agriculture and in human capital and circulate through the local region, and that the chan-neling of remittances into poor regions helps equilibrate national eco-nomic differences, the functionalists take a predominantly positive view of international migration.

Since 1982, the functionalist point of view has been emphasized in a series of studies that tend to be national or regional in scope. (Again, the Mexican literature is discussed in the next section.) Their conclusions stress the positive side of labor migration for sending areas. The functionalists directly counter the external dependency arguments of the structural school, contending that international migration actually frees migrants from dependency on traditional, "dead-end" jobs at the origin. Migration from the eastern Caribbean, for example, has enabled families to escape a declining, dependent plantation system with few prospects for the future (Conway 1985). For mainland Latin America, international migration substitutes one form of dependency (reliance on a fickle physical environment and ineffective government programs) for another (reliance on foreign economic and political conditions)—an orientation that may have a positive outcome for the migrating family, because the stability and reliability of conditions in the foreign country may exceed those at home.

In addition, the functionalists find evidence for an abundance of investments in small-scale projects and human capital, both of which increase household productivity. They argue that expenditures on health care and education should be considered not as consumption but as investment in human capital; even housing (particularly when the home is the workplace) can be categorized as a productivity-enhancing investment (Russell 1986). Small shops and services begun by migrants recirculate money in the community (Richardson 1983; Mendonsa 1982). Structuralists reveal their preoccupation with centrist, conventional development strategies when they deprecate the small, incremental projects undertaken by migrants; and of course, migrants may save in small increments until they accumulate enough to make major purchases and investments (Keely and Tran, 1989).

Another functionalist argument is that international migration may decrease inequalities, particularly at the regional and national scales. Because international migrants often come from the more rural, poorer areas of the country, their remittances improve the relative economic status of their villages in the larger space economy, even though intravillage inequalities may be increased. For example, land acquisitions by return migrants to Barbados in the late 1800s enabled the formation of independent rural communities; and in Nevis, shops financed with remittances allowed smaller communities to survive in the face of competition from nearby urban centers (Rubenstein 1982).

Finally, migrant remittances assist in generating positive trade balances for sending countries, which in turn enable them to acquire vital imports and to pay off foreign debts. Money is channeled into sending-area banks through compulsory remittance schemes as well as spontaneously; this becomes development capital for projects in the home country or region (Ling 1984; Morrison and Sinkin 1982; Kirwan 1981).

The functionalists are in fundamental disagreement with the structuralists, then, on the nature of dependency, the extent of migrant investments, and the equilibrating or disequilibrating effect of migrant remittances. There is some grudging agreement between the two schools, however. They agree that migrant families tend to be better off economically than nonmigrant families (excluding the local economic elite). They agree that international migration seldom generates true economic development at the origin. They appear to agree, on the positive side, that migration alleviates balance of payment problems, and on the negative side, that some social disintegration occurs as a result of migration. Nevertheless, the distance between the two perspectives underscores the need for a more encompassing theory on the impact of international migration on areas of origin.

Origin Impacts of Mexico–United States Migration
Localities of Village Impact Studies in Mexico

Research on the impacts of U.S. migration on towns and villages in central Mexico has been extensive in the nineteen years since Cornelius's classic study of the Los Altos region of Jalisco (Cornelius 1976). More than twenty different places have been studied—from larger towns to places with a few hundred inhabitants, in addition to a neighborhood in Guadalajara, Mexico's second-largest metropolitan area (Massey et al. 1987). Some of these studies deal primarily with topics other than economic and social impacts at the origin, such as migration networks and selectivity and migration history. However, they all touch upon origin impacts to some degree.

As the map shows (fig. 1.2), the spatial coverage by studies in Mexico has been quite uneven. Some three-fourths of the places studied are in two states—Jalisco and Michoacán—that lie at the southern margin of the "migrant hearth," which comprises the states indicated by the sand pattern with the exception of the northernmost three. The Los Altos region of Jalisco and the Bajío Zamorano/Lake Pátzcuaro regions of Michoacán have been the chief foci of these studies. The other one-fourth are in Guanajuato (Jones et al. 1984), Zacatecas (Mines 1981; Jones 1992a), Morelos (Grindle 1988), and Oaxaca (James and Kearney 1981). Jalisco and Michoacán represent well the west-central hearth area of current Mexican-U.S. migration, but these two states still account for only an estimated 27 percent of Mexico's undocumented migration in the early 1980s (Jones 1986). It is significant that important sending states such as Chihuahua, Baja California Norte, Coahuila, Durango, and the Distrito Federal (Mexico City) have not been the focus of any known origin impact studies.

What is the reason for this uneven coverage? Many writers justify their selection of sites in Michoacán and Jalisco with the argument that these

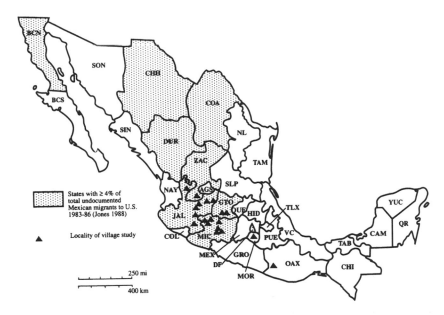

Figure 1.2 Localities of "village" studies of U.S. migration, 1976–1990 (*Mexican State Abbreviations*: AGS = Aguascalientes; BCN = Baja California Norte; BCS = Baja California Sur; CAM = Campeche; COA = Coahuila; COL = Colima; CHI = Chiapas; CHH = Chihuahua; DF = Distrito Federal; DUR = Durango; GTO = Guanajuato; GRO = Guerrero; HID = Hidalgo; JAL = Jalisco; MEX = Mexico; MIC = Michoacán; MOR = Morelos; NAY = Nayarit; NL = Nuevo León; OAX = Oaxaca; PUE = Puebla; QUE = Querétaro; QR = Quintana Roo; SLP = San Luis Potosí; SIN = Sinaloa; SON = Sonora; TAB = Tabasco; TLX = Tlaxcala; VC = Vera Cruz; YUC = Yucatán; ZAC = Zacatecas)

two states account for more migrants to the United States than any others, situated as they are in the traditional source region for this migration (Massey et al. 1987, 3). Furthermore, there is an inertial effect, by which past studies within this region induce follow-up studies (see, for example, Cornelius 1990). Finally, universities such as the Universidad Autónoma de Guadalajara, the Colegio de Jalisco, and the Colegio de Michoacán have developed special programs within which faculty and their students are continuously investigating migration in the region. Thus, there is a logical explanation for the focus on the west-central region. Furthermore, this research is very insightful and cumulatively enlightening. However, there is clearly great potential for the study of migration in other states and regions. Such research might modify some of our ideas about causal forces, patterns of flow, and impacts.

The Structural Perspective on Mexican Migration to the United States

The literature on origin impacts of Mexican migration to the United States parallels that on international migration in general with regard to points of view, spatial scales of analysis, timing, and conclusions. Before the mid-1980s, the structural arguments predominated.

Reichert (1981) eloquently presents the structuralist viewpoint in the quotation that opens this chapter, based upon his (and Massey's) case study of "Guadalupe," an anonymous town of 2,700 in northern Michoacán. Migrants develop an ever-growing dependency on foreign labor, not in order to promote productive family enterprises but to engage in consumption that increases their status in the community. This process grows upon itself, and families are forced to continue migrating in order to maintain the lifestyle to which they have become accustomed.

The tendency to disinvest in the local community is observed in many studies, and it has several dimensions. First, migrant families spend their new income on conspicuous consumption rather than on either private or public investments. Migrants from "Guadalupe" (Reichert 1981; see also Foster 1967) prided themselves on such purchases as home improvements, clothing and appliances, and the best medical care (to demonstrate their prosperity), weddings and drinking parties (to show their magnanimity), and land (not to work themselves but to rent out or to hold for later resale at a profit). In another Michoacán study, Dinerman (1982) found that as the village of Huecorio evolved into a migrant-sending area, contributions to community work *faenas* (family work quotas) declined and individual home improvements increased. A second dimension of disinvestment is migrants' tendency to make their consumption purchases externally rather than locally. For example, in Acuitzio del Canje, another Michoacán town (Wiest 1979, 1984), migrants spent most of their earnings in regional cities and industrial metropolises, on such items as clothing and appliances, construction material, medicine and medical care, banking, education, and rent paid to absentee property owners. Only a few purchases were made in the town—food and drink, transportation services, and payments to local landowners. A third component of disinvestment is the tendency for remittances to drop in an absolute sense as the branch family residing abroad grows in size and commitment to life in the United States (Mines 1981; see also Massey 1986; Cornelius 1990).

With respect to migration's effects on local labor markets, not many writers argue that skills acquired in the United States are irrelevant to rural

Mexico (in fact, many examples of the reverse can be cited). However, labor shortages may be created when migrants leave a local economy which is based in part on labor-intensive industries or commercial agriculture. In Gómez Farías, Michoacán, the seasonal flight of workers to the Central Valley of California leaves the local strawberry fields without hands to harvest the crop (López Castro 1986, 71). Shortages may also be created simply because returning or vacationing migrants do not wish to work at jobs that pay a fraction of what they pay in the United States (Mines 1981, 127).

Economic inequality, by which is usually meant income differences between families within the village, is one of the most noted by-products of U.S. migration. It is argued that migration and the remittances it brings entrench a social class that has more resources to begin with—not, perhaps, the highest-income families, but those who constitute a small, emergent upper middle class. This elite does not include all migrants but only those with superior experience and contacts. For example, an elite composed of legal migrants developed in "Guadalupe," Michoacán (Reichert 1981); this group had incomes and possessions far greater than those of the illegal migrant class. Another example is the Lake Pátzcuaro region of Michoacán (Dinerman 1982), and still another, the southern tip of Zacatecas (Mines 1981). In each of these cases, a dual class structure developed: on the one hand, a U.S.-based group of migrants who worked in semiskilled jobs in the United States and vacationed in the village; on the other, a village-based group composed of both nonmigrants and shuttle migrants who worked in temporary unskilled jobs in the United States. The village-based group sharecropped or worked at day labor in the village and earned, overall, only a fraction of the wages of the U.S.-based group. This economic structure was sustained by a social class structure based on kinship networks which reinforced the position of the U.S.-based group by providing financial support as well as job information and assistance in the United States.

Social disintegration is almost a foregone conclusion when an intensely family-oriented society loses its heads of household for months and years at a time; migrants with little education and low family status earn more money than the top professionals in the town; liberal lifestyles are injected by the migrants into a conservative community; and the level of goods and services available in the home community is compared with that available in U.S. towns and cities. Several dimensions of this problem are discussed at length by López Castro (1986) in his book *La Casa Dividida* (The

house divided). The migrant lives with "el sustento en un lado, y el cora-
zón en otro" ([his] sustenance on one side of the border, and [his] heart
on the other). Among returning youth, the phenomenon of *cholismo* (a
lifestyle, dress, and vocabulary typical of East Los Angeles, with its roots in
the Chicano protest movements of the 1940s) is being infused into small
rural communities like Gómez Farías (Michoacán). Cholismo also perpetu-
ates the positive myths about U.S. migration, inasmuch as the tribulations
of the migrants are painted in heroic terms. The *cholo* is usually very critical
of village life, and his presence creates cleavages between the older and
younger residents.

The Functional Perspective on Mexican Migration to the United States

Beginning in the mid-1980s, authors spread a wider net and often studied
several villages simultaneously and comparatively as well as focusing on regional and national impacts. Furthermore, interestingly, the world recession since then has reestablished wage-labor migration as an important
contributor to family welfare as well as to national balances of payments.
Positive views of the impacts of U.S. migration tend to dominate this more
recent research.

The implication by dependency theorists is that international migration
creates a situation of dependence and thus that U.S. migration may not be
the most rational strategy for migrants and their villages. Several functionalist writers suggest otherwise—in particular, Merilee Grindle (1988) in
the quotation that appears at the beginning of this chapter. Grindle suggests that the peasant from central Mexico faces less risk and uncertainty
from U.S. migration than from any other possible income-generating activity. (In this view, she is in clear agreement with Conway's [1985] views
on the eastern Caribbean). He risks more with the status quo—relying on
an unreliable resource base, a rigid local social structure, undependable
government programs, and uncertain job opportunities in other Mexican cities—than in seeking work in the United States. It would follow
from Grindle's argument that in many ways the migrant and the household are more autonomous for having chosen U.S. migration, not more
dependent.

Recent functionalist studies identify a number of examples of investment in the local community. From one-third to two-thirds of all businesses in small migrant communities of Michoacán and Jalisco were
begun with U.S. migrant earnings and are presently owned by migrants

(Cornelius 1990; Massey et al. 1987). These businesses tend to be small retail outlets, but they redistribute money locally and hire significant numbers of local workers. Moreover, in two agricultural communities (one south of Guadalajara, the other near Zamora, Michoacán) migrant experience clearly increased both the productivity of agriculture and its commercialization (Massey et al. 1987, chapter 8). Among long-term migrant families more hybrid seeds, fertilizers, and machinery were being used and more wage labor was being hired than among short-term migrants or nonmigrants (see Roberts 1982 for further support). This was happening at the same time that acreages were decreasing, so it is not certain from the data how total agricultural production was affected; however, it may be assumed that the less productive land was being taken out of production.

Even though migrant remittances fall short of inducing economic development, functionalists argue that they do generate economic growth at both the local and regional levels by the so-called multiplier effect, by which external earnings are recirculated within the local and regional economies. In a questionnaire survey of two villages in the Lake Pátzcuaro region, Adelman et al. (1988) found a relatively high local multiplier for migrant remittances. For every $100 increase in remittances, total community income increased by $188—a multiplier of 1.88. This is a very significant figure for a village; by comparison, small towns in the United States have export base multipliers of between 1.2 and 1.8 (Jones 1987; Garrison 1972; Weiss and Gooding 1968). It indicates that migrant families made a significant portion of their purchases in their villages. Even the amount that did leave the villages probably didn't go far. Other research illustrates this. Remittances entering Las Animas, Zacatecas; Tlaquitapa, Jalisco; and Chamitlán, Michoacán, were used to purchase goods and establish businesses in Nochistlán, Lagos de Moreno, and Zamora, respectively (Cornelius 1990, 69; Massey et al. 1987, chapter 8).

Regarding income inequalities, further economic analysis of the Lake Pátzcuaro data already discussed (Adelman et al. 1988) reveals several striking conclusions (Taylor 1987; Stark et al. 1986). In one village with a history of U.S. migration but little history of internal migration (to other places in Mexico) remittances from the United States tended to lessen inequalities, while internal remittances tended to increase them. This was true because U.S. dollars were funneled into families of below-average incomes, and this had a leveling effect on the income distribution; conversely, internal migrant remittances were directed toward families that were already better off. In another village, with a history of internal migration but little history of U.S. migration, just the reverse was found. That is, internal remittances redistributed village income to the lower classes, while U.S. remittances were directed to a relatively few families from the upper part of the income distribution. These conclusions are supported by an earlier study of Villa Guerrero, Jalisco (Shadow 1979), a community with substantial migration to the United States. U.S. migration tended to channel money to the lower half of the income distribution, while internal migration channeled money to the upper half.

U.S. migration thus emerges from these arguments as an income equalizer under certain conditions—namely, where it is the poorer families who practice it. It replaces the pronounced inequalities that have long existed in Mexican villages (Mines 1981, 106–8; de Walt 1979; Pi-Sunyer 1973; Fromm and Maccoby 1970; Lewis 1963) with a more egalitarian distribution of incomes.

Finally, functionalists have investigated the impacts of migrant remittances on regional and national balances of payments. In the mid-1970s an estimated $2 to $3 billion per year was being transferred to Mexico from the United States (Díez-Canedo 1984). These remittances constituted some 64 percent of the territorial product of the state of Zacatecas and 40 percent of that of Guanajuato. In the late 1970s, an average of $1,250 per migrant was returned to Mexico each year in the form of remittances (Ranney and Kossoudji 1983). Assuming only two million total remitters at that time (see Robinson 1980), this represents $2.5 billion in 1978, a figure consistent with that of Díez-Canedo. This represents the third (possibly the second) most important foreign-exchange earner for Mexico at that time, after petroleum and the maquiladoras, and far ahead of tourism.

Toward a Comprehensive Theory of Origin Impacts

The profound differences of opinion over whether international wage-labor migration benefits the sending society suggest that the question is very complex. In fact, the question may have no answer as stated, because whether the impact is positive or negative depends on the circumstances. Therefore, a better question is, Under what conditions does migration benefit the sending society, and under what conditions does it do harm?

The literature suggests that the impact of wage-labor migration on economic advancement at the origin depends on three controlling factors: the

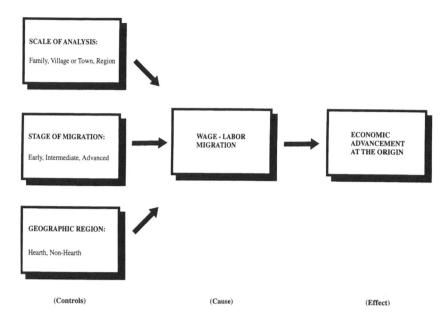

Figure 1.3 Factors controlling the impacts of wage-labor migration on the origin

scale of analysis, the stage of migration, and the particular geographic region (fig. 1.3). Migration may have a beneficial economic effect at one scale—the family scale, for example—while at another, perhaps the village scale, its effects are negative. Analogously, migration may heighten economic inequalities in a village that finds itself at an early stage of U.S. migration, whereas it may alleviate inequalities in a village at the intermediate stage. Thus, there are conditional factors which control the relationship between migration and economic advancement. Since the structuralists and functionalists tend to operate at different scales and in different regions, and to study different points in the migration process, their conclusions may in part be explained by these controlling factors. The study of migration from Mexico to the United States provides an extended example of how these three factors affect results.

Scale of Analysis

Consider first the sociospatial scale of analysis. Whether a study is carried out at the family, village, or regional level influences its conclusions about the economic benefits to Mexico of U.S. migration (table 1.1a). Studies carried out at the scale of the village (or town) have focused on community economic and social phenomena—productive enterprises of the extended family, relative levels of investment and consumption, local levels of employment and unemployment, community projects to which migrants contribute, the places where migrant families spend their money, and local social institutions such as the church. At this scale, they have concluded that migration leads to disinvestment in, and disintegration of, the community's economic and social institutions. By way of contrast, studies focusing on the economic welfare of the individual family and its members have found substantial economic improvement—although not necessarily social advancement. Studies at the broader, regional level have also come to positive conclusions, finding, for example, that migrant remittances are important generators of foreign exchange earnings. The parabolic nature of the benefit/disbenefit ratio with respect to change in the sociospatial scale of

Table 1.1 Factors Controlling the Impact of U.S. Migration on Local Advancement in Mexico

Control	Control Attribute	Relationship between U.S. Migration and Indicator for Economic Advancement	Perspective: S=Structural F=Functional
a. Scale of Analysis	Family:	US Mig. → Econ. Improvement	F
	Village/Town:	US Mig. → Econ. Decline	S
	Region:	US Mig. → Econ. Improvement	F
b. Scale of Analysis	Family:		na
	Village/Town:	US Mig. → Increasing Fam. Income Ineqs.	S
	Region:	US Mig. → Decreasing Fam. Income Ineqs.	F
c. Scale of Analysis	Family:	US Mig. → Local Expenditures	S, F
	Village/Town:	US Mig. → Non-Local Expenditures	S
	Region:	US Mig. → Local Expenditures	F
d. Stage of Migration (Family)	Early:	US Mig. → Consumption	S
	Intermediate:	US Mig. → Consumption, Investment	S, F
	Advanced:	US Mig. → Consumption, Investment	S, F
e. Stage of Migration (Family)	Early:	US Mig. → Local Expenditures	F
	Intermediate:	US Mig. → Local & Non-Local Expends.	S, F
	Advanced:	US Mig. → Non-Local Expenditures	S
f. Stage of Migration (Town, Village)	Early:	US Mig. → Increasing Fam. Income Ineqs.	S
	Intermediate:	US Mig. → Decreasing Fam. Income Ineqs.	F
	Advanced:	US Mig. → Increasing Fam. Income Ineqs.	S
g. Geographic Region	Hearth:	US Mig. → Econ. Improvement/Decline	F, S
	Non-Hearth:	US Mig. → Small Impact on Either	F, S

na = not applicable

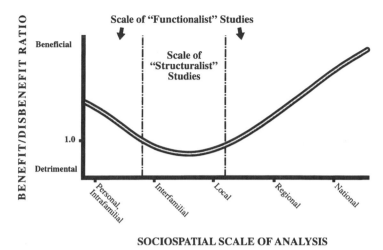

Figure 1.4 How the scale of analysis affects origin impacts of international migration (ratio is hypothetical)

analysis is shown graphically in figure 1.4. Note that the functionalists have tended to carry out research at the smaller and larger scales, and the structuralists, at the intermediate scales. This tendency helps to explain their respective conclusions.

A well-reasoned version of the functionalist argument of U.S. migration's positive impacts at the regional scale is provided by community economic base analysis (Tiebout 1962). This type of analysis traces the flow of basic income (that deriving from external purchasers of local goods and services) through the many nonbasic sectors of the local economy (the local wholesale, retail, and service businesses that cater to local needs). It can thus be used to show the impacts on a community's growth of each of several types of external income and to compare these impacts across a number of communities (Garrison 1972; Weiss and Gooding 1968; Jones 1991). U.S. migration is just such a basic income source for rural north-central Mexico, but there are others: internal migration, external commuting to jobs in cities of the local region, commercial agriculture, private businesses and industries, and federal and state government payrolls and investments (fig. 1.5). The sale of such goods and services to outsiders provides the "fuel" to run the local economic engine; these sales depend, in turn, on the special comparative advantages of the community and its population vis-à-vis other communities. However, these sales mean little if the money earned by the migrants, commuters, farmers, businessmen, and others is spent outside of the community—that is, if the "fuel" leaks away before reaching the engine. Thus, income recycling within the community—the oft-cited multiplier effect—is critical for local growth. This income recycling is itself a function of the community's population, location, labor force structure, and migration history (fig. 1.5).

The scale of a study also influences its conclusions about inequalities (table 1.1b). No known studies adopt the family scale of analysis (i.e., looking at income inequalities among members of a family due to migration), but several structuralist studies have been conducted at the level of the village or town (looking at income differences among families). They have invariably found that U.S. migration steepens the income gradient between rich and poor families, creating an ever-widening, "disequilibrating" gap between the migrant "haves" and the nonmigrant "have-nots" (fig. 1.6a). Studies at the regional scale (looking at family income differences among towns or between rural and urban areas) are quite scarce. They spring from the functionalist school and support an opposite conclusion: U.S. migration lessens the income gradient by redistributing income from large to small towns. The reason is quite simple: in Mexico, U.S. migration rates are higher in small towns than in large towns and cities. Thus, migrant remittances are channeled into the towns at far higher rates than into the

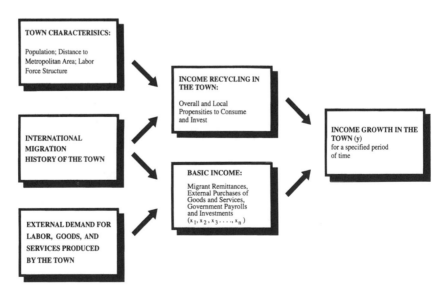

Figure 1.5 A small-town economic base model incorporating international migration

a. Disequilibration   **b. Equilibration**

UNIT: FAMILY (within town or   UNIT: TOWN (between towns,
      rural area)   or between rural and urban area)

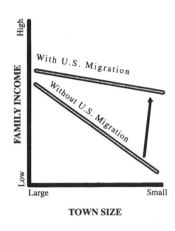

Figure 1.6 Family income gradients by spatial unit of analysis

cities. Since small towns are often destitute while cities are better off, U.S. migration serves as an "equilibrating" mechanism at this scale (fig. 1.6b). Finally, the scale of a study clearly influences its conclusions about the externalization of expenditures—that is, about the places where local migrant families spend their money (table 1.1c). Considering the family as the unit of analysis, many studies from both the structural and the functional perspectives conclude that proceeds from U.S. migration tend to stay within the nuclear family (that is, they are spent "locally"; see, e.g., Mines 1981). Studies at the village scale, dominated by the structuralists, argue that most remittances leak away from the town into nearby metropolitan economies, or to the United States, and are lost to the community (e.g., Wiest 1984). Functional studies taking a larger regional perspective (e.g., Díez-Canedo 1984; Adelman et al. 1988) see considerable recirculation of remittances within their regions of destination.

Stage of Migration

Consider next the stage of migration. The literature suggests that a family which has just begun sending migrants will spend its remittances differently from a family which has done so for years. Specifically, the relative magnitudes of consumption and investment will differ (table 1.1d). This brings up another question unanswered in the literature—just what constitutes consumption and investment? Items such as food, clothing, appliances, and furniture would be accepted by most as representing consumption, in that they fulfill immediate family needs and enhance the family's economic and perhaps its social status. At the other extreme, the purchase of agricultural inputs (animals, land, seed, fertilizers, insecticides, machinery and tools), a truck, a piece of land, or the establishment of a family business would be considered by most to represent investment. But in between are a wide array of expenditures that cannot be conclusively identified as either consumption or investment. Contributions to church and community projects, for example, serve as conspicuous expenditures to enhance the family's social status and also as social investment in the community. Education and medical care may be considered consumption (they fulfill immediate family needs) as well as investment in human capital (they augment the long-term productivity of the family). Home improvements may better the family's immediate quality of life and prestige, or increase its income-earning potential by enabling a family member to work at home. Interest may represent payments on a loan for either consumption or investment purposes. Because family expenditures on church, community, education, medical care, housing, and interest may have components of both types, I categorize them as mixed consumption and investment expenditures.

Given these definitions, we may surmise from the literature that a family in the early stage of migration spends primarily on consumption (table 1.1d; figure 1.7). The family is generally poor and must spend much of its new income on food, along with small consumer durable items and clothing. A family in an intermediate stage has accumulated several years of experience and remittances and is able to give more to the community, to afford better schools and specialized medical care, and to make home improvements. These expenditures may be characterized as a mixture of consumption and investment. Finally, a family in the advanced stage of migration has cumulated enough remittances to invest in a truck, a piece of agricultural machinery, or a parcel of land. At the same time, this family may spend money on consumer goods such as major appliances and perhaps an automobile. Therefore, both major consumption and major investment goods are targeted in this final stage. Not only do families progress from one category of expenditure to another, but within each category they progress from the smaller, piecemeal items, to the larger, "lumpy" (requiring a lump-sum expenditure) items.

The family's stage of migration also influences where these expenditures are made (table 1.1e). Consumption expenditures, which characterize the early stage, tend to be made locally—particularly food, whose perishability tends to mitigate against its purchase outside of town. Increasing externalization of family expenditures accompanies the later stages, however. With increased U.S. migration experience, the family purchases more consumption and investment goods in the United States. In the most advanced stages, members of the family live in the United States and naturally most of their expenditures are there. When purchasing goods in Mexico, the family prefers higher-quality goods and is able to afford the transportation to shop for them in larger towns and cities. Some items are available only in these larger places. Thus, the propensity to spend in the local town or village, for all types of goods, declines with U.S. migration experience. Structuralists have tended to focus on the advanced stages of migration while functionalists have focused on the intermediate stages; this helps to explain why structuralists see a strong externalization of expenditures while functionalists do not.

Consider now the stage of migration not of the family but of the town. In diffusion theory, the adoption of an innovation (e.g., hybrid corn, hula

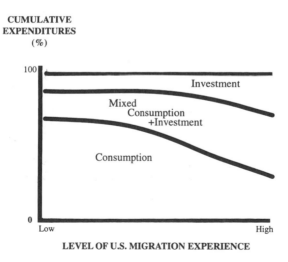

Figure 1.7 Family expenditures and U.S. migration experience

hoops, cable television, or the decision to migrate) among people in a place follows a well-known pattern (Brown 1981; Rogers 1983; Morrill et al. 1988). Adoption is slow at first, involving a very few well-educated or risk-taking persons—the innovators. Later, adoption becomes more contagious, accelerating during the early adopter phase and then decelerating in the late adopter stage, until ultimately most people have adopted the innovation, save for a few holdouts—the laggards. A given community may find itself at any point along this adoption continuum. The decision to migrate to the United States diffuses among persons in a central Mexican town in just this fashion.

The special concern here is how the town's stage of migration determines whether further U.S. migration will increase or decrease economic inequalities in the town (table 1.1f)—a question of critical importance in the literature, which suggests that U.S. migrants come from different parts of the income distribution of a town depending on its stage of migration adoption (fig. 1.8). In the *innovator stage* (fig. 1.8a), before any significant migration from the town, only the most ambitious and adventuresome residents make the trip, and these migrants come from a small number of families that are already fairly well off. Income inequalities in the town are increasing as a result of migration at this stage. In the *early adopter stage* (fig. 1.8b), migration has diffused down the bell-shaped curve, via communications between the innovators and other residents, and income inequalities are decreasing because the poorer families are now participating.

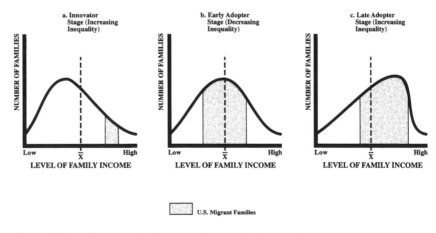

Figure 1.8 Family income distribution and stage of U.S. migration

In the *late adopter stage* (fig. 1.8c), continued U.S. migration creates a migrant class which stands increasingly apart from the "laggard" nonmigrant class. Income inequalities are once more increasing. This diffusional schema may help to explain some of the disparate conclusions presented by the structuralists and the functionalists. For example, from the structural perspective, Mines's (1981) and Dinerman's (1982) observation that migrants are initially drawn from upper-middle-class families with the money to support them, suggests the innovator stage. The functionalist conclusions of Stark, Taylor, and Yitzhaki (1986) on lessening of inequalities suggest the early adopter stage; and the structuralist conclusions of Reichert (1981) on the "migrant syndrome" support the late adopter stage of the model. See also table 1.1f, in which the early, intermediate, and advanced stages roughly correspond to the innovator, early adopter, and late adopter stages of figure 1.8.

Geographic Region

Finally, the geographic region chosen for analysis will affect the conclusions (table 1.1g). The traditional hearth region for U.S. migration, including Zacatecas, has few economically basic activities apart from U.S. migration. Thus, the role of migration there must be a strong one—either positive or negative depending on whether one believes the arguments of the functionalists or the structuralists. The non-hearth area, including Coahuila, is more dynamic, with economically basic activities such as trade, tourism, commercial agriculture, energy, and industry. Here, the role of migration in economic improvement or decline, we might expect, would be relatively small.

The foregoing discussion provides the theoretical framework for this book. This framework specifies the conditions under which U.S. migration would have positive or negative impacts on the area of origin in Mexico. Testing the effects of migration under these different conditions is one goal of this book.

Study Design

A full discussion of the reasoning behind the choice of study area, the sampling frame, and the survey research methodology is included as

Figure 1.9 Municipios of study (underlined) and nearby metropolitan municipios

appendix A. A brief summary follows. The two subregions chosen for study are central Zacatecas and northern Coahuila (fig. 1.9). Within each of these subregions, particular municipios were selected based upon their proximity to a metropolitan area and their representation of both smaller agricultural places and larger urbanized places. Within the municipios, towns and households were selected for interviewing using a random procedure (except that the *cabecera*, or municipio capital, was always included). Interviews were carried out by three binational teams during January through June of 1988. The household interview schedule (appendix B) included questions about demographic and economic characteristics of the household, the migration history (Mexican, U.S.) of all family members, purchases and expenses of the household, support of community institutions, and opinions of the respondent on the advantages and disadvantages of U.S. migration to the town and on what the town needs to improve economically. This provides the basis for the descriptions, analyses, and case studies of chapters 2 through 5. In all, 596 household questionnaires were completed in central Zacatecas, and 466 in northern Coahuila. In some of the towns, a questionnaire was administered to a sample of public and private establishments (appendix C); this information provides the foundation for the economic base analysis of Zacatecas in chapter 6.

Conclusions

The literature on the impacts of U.S. migration on Mexico is a microcosm of the broader literature that deals with origin impacts involving migration from Middle America and Asia to the United States, from southern Europe and North Africa to northern Europe, and from Asia to the Persian Gulf. Some authors see predominantly negative impacts; others, predominantly positive impacts.

The differences of opinion on Mexican impacts are basically a function of three factors—the sociospatial scale of analysis, the stage of migration, and the geographic region of study. The structural school, writing from a dependency or political economy perspective, has tended to study socioeconomic institutions at the village scale, in localities at advanced stages of U.S. migration, in the hearth region of central Mexico. Their conclusions have emphasized economic decline, increasing inequalities, consumption as opposed to investment, externalization of expenditures, and social disintegration. The functional school, writing from a microeconomic or macroeconomic perspective, has tended to examine either the individual family economy or the regional economy, in villages and towns at intermediate stages of U.S. migration, in the hearth region and elsewhere. Their conclusions have emphasized economic improvement, decreasing inequalities, reinvestment, and the recycling of U.S. remittances in the local region which encompasses the village.

This book is devoted, in part, to broadening the base of conclusions concerning the impacts of U.S. migration by surveying a range of places of differing sizes, at different stages of U.S. migration, and in two distinct subregions—central Zacatecas and northern Coahuila—that have been little studied in the past. Interviews with more than one thousand households in these two subregions in the first half of 1988 provide the substantive information which constitutes the core of the book.

2

The Context of Migration
Zacatecas and Coahuila

Zacatecas and much of Coahuila lie on the southern margin of the semi-arid Northern Plateau, or Mesa del Norte, region of Mexico, between and including parts of the Sierra Madres Oriental and Occidental (fig. 2.1). The Mesa del Norte, an elevated tableland, is the result of two massive tectonic forces—to the southwest, vulcanism (upwelling of molten rock), and to the northeast, diastrophism (folding and faulting of rock layers); both are associated with the inexorable westward movement of the North American plate. These forces have been particularly strong during the past 70 million years, a period referred to geologically as the Cenozoic. The Mesa del Norte is best visualized as a gigantic tilted table 400 miles wide and 600 miles long. At its southern margin, near the city of Zacatecas, it is 8,000 feet above sea level; in the northeast, it is only 2,000 feet high at Monclova. The mesa is also higher (by some 2,000 feet) at its western than at its eastern margin. Its southern margin is the boundary of the Mesa Central—a series of high, fertile basins surrounded by volcanic peaks. Its eastern margin is the Sierra Madre Oriental, which continues into the Big Bend area of Texas and on to the Front Range of the Rockies; its western margin, the Sierra Madre Occidental, continues into the interior Rocky Mountains west of the Colorado and Wasatch Plateaus.

Northeast of Monclova, the Mesa del Norte gives way to the Gulf Coastal Plain. This area benefits from the existence of artesian springs, which offer the possibility of irrigated agriculture, and from the fertile soils along its major rivers.

The two states share dry climates with hot summers and often cold winters. Both have mineral wealth that has been their salvation as well as their downfall. Both were important in the Mexican Revolution—Zacatecas as a sort of stamping ground for the opposing armies, and Coahuila as the intellectual cradle for the revolution. All of these factors—physical, historical, political—have been ultimately responsible for sending migrants in search of work in the United States. On the Northern Plateau these two states, along with Chihuahua, are the most important sending areas for wage-labor migration to the United States.

The broad similarities mentioned above conceal a number of important differences. For example, Zacatecas lies in the "hollow core" region of central Mexico (Jones 1988)—a region of limited economic potential at the northern border of the Indian-mestizo south (West and Augelli 1989, 340). Coahuila, on the other hand, lies in a dynamic border region solidly within the European-mestizo north. Its economic base includes heavy industry and power plants, maquiladoras, and commercial agriculture. Coahuila's high U.S. migration rate reflects both cyclical displacements due to economic downturns in an otherwise dynamic region and long-standing family ties that have facilitated travel to the United States. These differences will be discussed in this chapter.

Central Zacatecas

Central Zacatecas lies in the Sierra Madre Occidental, at the southern extremity of the Mesa del Norte (fig. 2.1). It is a series of basins and ranges

Figure 2.1 Physiographic and urban features of north-central Mexico

extending both southwestward and southeastward from the city of Zacatecas into the two protuberances known as the "feet" of the state. The basins range from 4,000 to 6,500 feet (1,219–1,981 m) high. Running southwestward from Zacatecas toward Guadalajara, in valleys between spurs of the Sierra Madre Occidental, lie the cities of Villanueva, at 6,200 feet (1,890 m) on the Agua Blanca River, and Jerez, at 6,600 feet (2,012 m) on the Colotlán (fig. 2.2). Mountains to the west reach some 9,000 feet (2,743 m). The soils of these valleys, from decomposed igneous sediments, are relatively fertile. To the southeast, on a broad floodplain opening toward Aguascalientes, at 6,100 feet (1,859 m) lies the town of Luis Moya, on even more fertile soils. The state capital, Zacatecas, sits perched at 7,900 (2,408 m) feet on a topographic divide amid volcanic hills; the area has little agricultural potential. However, the hills around

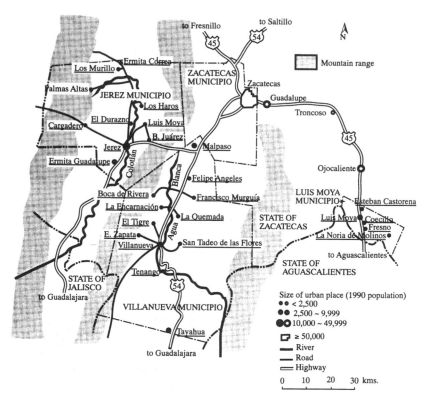

Figure 2.2 Central Zacatecas: Municipios and towns of study (sampled towns are underlined)

(and under) it contain veins of silver, lead, gold, and copper (*Síntesis Geográfica de Zacatecas* 1981). The climate of the region is subtropical steppe (BS in the Köppen system), with a concentration of rainfall in the summer months and little variation (15° F, or 8.3° C) between the hottest and coldest months. Lying in the rain shadow of mountains to the east, the region as a whole receives only 22–24 inches (56–61 cm) of rainfall per year—compared to nearly three times that in Tampico, at the same latitude on the Gulf coast (West and Augelli 1989, 43–47). Because of the semiarid climate, scrub vegetation—spiny shrubs (deciduous in the dry season), acacia, prickly pear and other cacti—prevails (*Síntesis Geográfica de Zacatecas* 1981).

The physical environment of central Zacatecas offers a partial, but not completely satisfactory, explanation for the high rates of emigration from the state. Despite the steppe climate and spiny vegetation, the region has fertile soils along the rivers, and in the mountains are minerals, natural grasses, and forests. There is no obvious physical reason why subsistence crop and livestock farming prevails here, instead of commercial grain farming, forestry, and horticulture, as in, say, northeastern New Mexico. The explanation of emigration from Zacatecas lies also in its history and its politics.

Historical Forces

Central Zacatecas shared in many of the events of the state's tumultuous past. As early as 20,000 years ago, paleo-Indians hunted in the region. These were supplanted around 6000 B.C. by seminomadic hunters and gatherers who moved down the intermontaine plateau into central Mexico, evolving into the Classical Mesoamerican civilizations. During the latter Classic and early post-Classic periods (specifically, from A.D. 540 to A.D. 1200), the culture referred to as Chicomostoc (La Quemada) flourished. Related to and tributary to the Toltecs, this group built an elaborate ceremonial center in the mountains above Villanueva, including a palace with columns, a central pyramid, and a fortress or citadel. A causeway headed southward, the beginning of a road that shipped turquoise to Tula, the Toltec capital. Chicomostoc was abandoned with the fall of the Toltecs around 1200. When the Spanish arrived, they found primitive groups such as the Zacatecos inhabiting the region, which was at the southern margin of the Gran Chichimeca, the region of uncivilized, nomadic tribes inhabiting much of northern Mexico (Secretaria de Educación Pública, México, 1982, 50–53).

During the preindependence period, the interests of the Spanish in Zacatecas were pacification, mineral exploitation, and agriculture to support
the silver and gold mines. Zacatecas was the "cradle of northward penetra-
tion into the Gran Chichimeca" (Secretaria de Educación Pública, México,
1982, 73). In the Juchipila area of southern Zacatecas, the Caxcanes (a
Zacateco group) were defeated by the Spanish in 1541, in response to their
raids on the newly established city of Guadalajara. Hearing of silver and
gold to the north, their perpetual siren call, the Spanish established the city
of Zacatecas in 1546, opening silver mines nearby and, soon afterward,
over the whole state. The needs of the mines led to lumbering in the western pine forests and, below them, cattle grazing. In the valley around Jerez,
grains were produced to provide food for the miners. Central Zacatecas
reached its economic prime in the mid-1700s, with more than a hundred
ore-reduction plants and some one-fifth of the world's total silver production. Already, however, the forests and pastures of Zacatecas were being
ruinously depleted, and silver discoveries elsewhere threatened the region's
hegemony.

In the period from independence to revolution, Zacatecas's economic
fortunes waxed and waned. In 1811, at the beginning of the independence
movement, Hidalgo's insurgents retreated northward across Zacatecas,
fleeing the advancing Spanish troops. After ten years of struggle, the mines,
agriculture, and cattle estates of Zacatecas had effectively stopped production. During the period between 1821 and 1910, however, the state recovered—more or less, according to the source one consults. Cross and
Sandos (1981) argue that in Zacatecas (and San Luis Potosí) under the
Porfiriato, the hacienda became "a vital premodern economic institution"
(p. 14). Highland production of wheat, corn, maguey, sheep, and cattle,
and lowland production of sugar, fruits, and fibers, were economically prof-
itable; nearly full employment and an absence of debt peonage were the
rule. In contrast, Cardoso (1980) argues that enforcement of the decree of
1857 disallowing the ownership of land by communal villages, which led
to the purchase and expropriation of this land by haciendas, resulted in a
stagnation of production, widespread debt peonage, and large-scale unemployment. Whichever argument we accept, it is certain that Zacatecas
sent many migrants north during the several decades prior to the revolution. In 1900, the central states (including the north-central states plus
Mexico, Puebla, and Hidalgo) had more than 600,000 migrants working
outside the region, chiefly in northern Mexico (Corwin 1978, 41).

The Mexican Revolution and its aftermath brought economic collapse to the state of Zacatecas. If independence brought production to a temporary halt, revolution destroyed productive capital and land so that production was decimated for years to come. After the Maderistas entered the capital in 1910, supportive insurgent troops under Luis Moya and Panfilo Natera marched southward taking Nieves, Fresnillo, Zacatecas, Jalpa, and Juchipila (*Enciclopedia de México* 1977, 1062–66; *Diccionario Porrva: Historia, Biografía, y Geografía de México* 1964, 3213). These troops ravaged the state (and the north-central region) by seizing grain and cattle and burning fields and manufacturing plants (e.g., sugar mills in the lowlands and maguey plants in the highlands) (Cross and Sandos 1981, 6–8). The mines were abandoned, and they flooded with water. Over the period 1910–16, the northward movement of federal troops, followed by the southward retaliations of insurgents such as Natera and Villa, turned Zacatecas into a wasteland. Agriculture was extinguished, mining paralyzed, and industry and commerce bankrupted. Nor were matters helped by a three-year drought (1915–17) that profoundly affected southern Zacatecas (Lozano et al. 1985).

There was little respite after the cessation of fighting in 1921. The Cristeros Rebellion (1926–29), a peasant revolt in reaction to anticlerical clauses in the Constitution of 1917, brought the Mexican army to the region, and further bloodshed and economic disaster ensued. Then, land reform, somewhat late to reach Zacatecas, arrived with a vengeance. The expropriation of hacienda land and the creation of ejidos (collective farms) doubled over the 1930s, aimed precisely at the north-central areas where the Cristeros had been most active. However, government support programs—credit, extension, seeds—were nonexistent or benefited only certain farms. As a result, productivity and employment dropped; wage rates for agricultural day labor in Zacatecas were a hundred times lower than those in California at the time (Cross and Sandos 1981, 12). Over this period, one-fifth of the population of the west-central region moved out permanently, to Mexico City, to northern Mexico, and to the United States (Cross and Sandos 1981, 9–10). Their opportunities improved with the latitude. In northern Mexico, jobs in Torreón, Monterrey, and border cities attracted them. Across the U.S. border, emerging irrigated agricultural operations in Texas and California and factories in San Antonio, Chicago, and other cities recruited almost exclusively Mexican labor, while the political climate in the United States supported the practice.

The period from 1940 to 1965, except for a short time during the 1950s, saw a continuation of the relative economic decline of Zacatecas.

This period was one of dramatic yield advances due to the green revolution, but Zacatecas saw little of this change, which was concentrated on the large collective wheat farms of Sonora and the cotton farms of La Laguna, Coahuila, and not on the individual ejidos. As Cross and Sandos (1981, 25) put it (paraphrasing Simpson 1937), "migration, not the ejido, proved to be 'Mexico's way out.' " Indeed, during the bracero program (1942–66), the Mexican government allocated some 50 percent of the total bracero contracts to the north-central region, which at that time had only 25 percent of the Mexican population. This was a tacit acknowledgment that the ejido could not solve the region's problems. In addition, it was probably an appeasement to the Sinarquistas, a political group that questioned the validity of the Mexican Revolution on both economic and religious grounds. The movement was centered in Guanajuato and had strong support across the north-central region (Cross and Sandos 1981, 35–48).

Post-1965 Zacatecas has been, as before, the victim of political forces beyond its control. Government price supports, particularly under Echeverría (1970–76), favored domestic corn production over imports, but by then the country faced recession, inflation, and a dramatic slowdown of growth in gross domestic product, all of which more than countered any gains from this policy. At the same time, oil-based inputs were driving up the cost of production. After Echeverría, the government's long-standing attitude—that low food prices for urban consumers were more important than high prices for farmers—returned (Cross and Sandos 1981, 62–69). As a result, during the 1970s and 1980s, most of the agricultural household heads in the state were underemployed. It is not surprising that Zacatecas's share of the total Mexican migrants to the United States rose from around 5 percent in the period from 1920 to 1940 (Gamio 1930; Whetten 1948), to some 8 percent in subsequent decades (Hancock 1959; Samora 1971; North and Houstoun 1976; Jones 1986). Nor is it surprising that such migrants today are of predominantly rural origins. Despite some improvements in the 1980s in mining and in commercial fruit and vegetable production, the large bulk of rural residents live in the same dismal economic circumstances that have prevailed since the revolution.

The Economy Today

Central Zacatecas, like the rest of the state, depends on the extraction of resources for its livelihood. A decade ago, almost two-thirds of the labor force of Zacatecas worked in agriculture and mining, and only one-third in the secondary and tertiary sectors (INEGI, *Integración Territorial*, 1980). Today, the figures are closer to one-half in each. For Texas, by comparison, in the early 1980s over two-thirds worked in the tertiary sector alone (Jordan et al. 1984).

There were bright spots in the Zacatecas economy in the 1980s. With the world recession, silver prices rose; in fact, silver accounted for 35 percent of Mexico's nonfuel exports in 1985 (West and Augelli 1989), and today Mexico leads the world in silver production (Espenshade 1990). And as Mexico leads the world, so Zacatecas leads Mexico. Important silver deposits are found all across the state, from north (Mazapil) to south (Pinos) and from east (Zacatecas and Fresnillo) to west (Sain Alto, Sombrerete). These are combined with zinc and lead, which are also commercially important (Mexico is fifth in world production of each). Mining productivity has increased over the past few decades, with remote-control explosives, electric drills, and special loaders and transporters enabling one miner to do the work that five did before. In the early 1980s, despite providing only 2 percent of the jobs in Zacatecas, mining directly generated 11 percent of the state's income. Agriculture suffered from the reverse condition (63 percent of the labor force earned only 23 percent of the income). However, in central and southern Zacatecas, a bright spot is the emergence of commercial fruit and vegetable farming in areas such as Jerez (peaches), Luis Moya (grapes), and Jalpa (guavas). It is for this reason that fruits now account for one-fifth of Zacatecas's total agricultural production by value (Secretaria de Educación Pública, México, 1982, 203–5).

Nevertheless, mining is subject to the whims of the world market, and agriculture is still dominated by dryland corn and beans (which together account for 90 percent of the state's crop acreage; see *Zacatecas: Cuaderno de Información para la Planeación* 1986), which are subject to the whims of the weather. Owing to drought, the years 1987 and 1978 saw effectively no production of corn and beans in the state. Most of the manufacturing sector in Zacatecas is tied to resource extraction and processing—ore concentration, food processing, and bottling. In the case of commercial fruit and vegetable production, the major portion of value added occurs after these products leave the state. Recently, silver mines have closed in the state, and staple crop agriculture has been further eroded with the prospect of free trade. If internal colonialism exists in Mexico, it is well illustrated in the case of Zacatecas, where the relative decline in the prices for its commodities, coupled with its dependence on decisions made outside the region, constrains economic growth.

Table 2.1 Selected Socioeconomic Indicators: Mexico and Central Zacatecas, 1990

Indicator	Mexico	Total, 3 mcpos	Luis Moya	Villa-nueva	Jerez	Zacatecas mcpo. (for comparison)
		Study Municipios in Central Zacatecas				
Population (thousands)	81,250	104.8	11.5	35.4	58.0	108.6
Population growth, 1980–1990 (%)	21.5	4.7	22.4	−0.6	5.1	22.2
Sex ratio (males per 100 females)	96.5	91.5	98.9	92.7	89.3	94.4
% urban (places of 5,000+ pop.)	65.6	46.3	46.7	25.2	59.2	92.2
% labor force in agriculture	23.5	41.8	41.9	51.0	35.8	4.8
% labor force in manufacturing	19.9	10.6	16.9	6.9	11.4	9.1
Median monthly income (1990 pesos, thousands)	416	318	341	277	330	448
Median monthly income (1990 U.S. dollars)[a]	154	118	126	103	122	166
Inequality of income[b]	1.067	1.438	.982	1.640	1.368	.975
No. of migrants per 1,000 residents[c]	2.8	12.3	4.4	13.7	12.8	20.1[d]

Source: *X Censo General de Población y Vivienda*, 1990, unless otherwise indicated.
a. Converted at a rate of 2,700 pesos to the dollar (mid-1990).
b. Standardized quartile deviation, defined as $(Q_3 - Q_1)/Md$, where Q_3, Q_1 = third and first income quartiles, respectively, and Md is the median.
c. Based on Immigration and Naturalization Service I-213 forms (Jones 1988).
d. Unnaturally inflated due to tendency for INS aprehendees to give closest metropolitan area as their previous residence. Based on 1980 populations (see Jones 1988).

A demographic and economic profile (table 2.1) shows that the study municipios are below the national average in socioeconomic status. Not only is the region's median income per labor force member relatively low (about three-fourths of the national average), but income is more unequally distributed, as indicated by the income inequality figure in table 2.1. In addition, a relatively large proportion of the labor force is still in agriculture and a small proportion in manufacturing, and a relatively small proportion lives in urban areas. Population growth is low (less than one-fourth the national average), which can be explained by the outmigration of men in their reproductive years and the concomitant lack of in-migration. Completing this profile is the rate of migration to the United States, which is over four times the national average. Although not shown in the table, internal migration is also prevalent, and colonies of central Zacatecanos are found in Mexico City, Guadalajara, Monterrey, Saltillo, Tijuana, Mexicali, and Ciudad Juárez. Finally, the municipio of Zacatecas (the state capital) is included for comparison. Note that it is quite urban, economically well-off, and fast growing, compared to the nonmetropolitan municipios. As the regional growth center, it benefits from the agglomeration of capital, industry, services, and government; it is proximate to but a world apart from the rural areas of Villanueva or Jerez municipios.

The Study Municipios

The three nonmetropolitan municipios that are the focus of this study represent some of the variety of the central Zacatecas region. Zacatecas, the capital and largest city, is excluded from the migration and impact analyses in chapters 3, 4, 5, and 6, owing to its very different character. However, here its demographic and migration characteristics are discussed briefly.

Luis Moya (named for the revolutionary leader from Sombrerete, Zacatecas) is a small municipio whose county seat is located 40 miles southeast of Zacatecas on Federal Highway 45 (fig. 2.2). Luis Moya thrives on commercial agriculture. Leaving the capital city at almost 8,000 feet (2,438 m) and descending southward, one enters a broad plain that reaches 10 miles (16 km) in width at the town of Luis Moya (population 5,366 in 1990), the midpoint on the road to Aguascalientes. The town is much more tied to Aguascalientes than to Zacatecas, in terms of its trade as well as its agriculture and processing industries. At around 6,200 feet (1,890 m), the town sits atop an aquifer which enables widespread irrigation of the floodplain. The area is noted for its garlic, which is exported to the U.S.; its chiles and onions; and, westward in the foothills of the Sierra Fría, grapes for the famed Pedro Domeq wines. Most of this production is on private lands. The municipio is dynamic, as evidenced by its high population growth rate (table 2.1). Additional evidence for this dynamism is provided by its many small apparel plants, which produce jeans for metropolitan markets to the south. These are internal *maquiladoras*, in which the material is shipped in, the cutwork and sewing performed locally, and the product shipped out. This industry got its start from migrants who worked in large apparel plants in Mexico City, Guadalajara, and Monterrey, then returned to their home towns to start their own small industries. The internal maquiladoras have spawned garment plants that are now exporting to the United States. It is not too surprising that Luis Moya sends comparatively few migrants to the United States in comparison to the rest of its region. Its location and physical geography have conspired to provide it with endogenous opportunities, despite its small size and strongly agricultural orientation.

Villanueva municipio is a very different sort of place—one chiefly devoted to subsistence agriculture. It is also agricultural, at about the same elevation as Luis Moya, and some 40 miles (64 km) from Zacatecas (to the southwest on Federal Route 54 to Guadalajara; see fig. 2.2). However, it is located astraddle a narrower river valley than Luis Moya's, between spurs of the Sierra Madre Occidental, whose peaks reach some 8,000 feet (2,438 m) in elevation. The rural population lives in hamlets and small towns scattered in the foothills, on the mesas, and up the canyons that make up much of the topography of this large municipio (835 square miles). Groundwater in these locations is deep and expensive to exploit. Surface reservoirs do exist, but only at the far southern and northern extremities of the municipio. Because of both physical geography and population distribution, water supply is a chronic problem. Agriculture is chiefly dryland corn and beans. Compared to nearby municipios such as Luis Moya and Jerez, Villanueva has scant irrigated acreage and only small fledgling experiments in grapes, peaches, apples, and tilapia farming. Not surprisingly, population growth is low, and incomes are the lowest in the region. Furthermore, because this is a dual society of rural peasants and urban merchants and politicians (the latter two chiefly in the city of Villanueva, which had 8,906 people in 1990), the municipio has a high index of income inequality (table 2.1).

This description suggests that the municipio's problems may not be attributed entirely to its physical geography. The political leadership of Villanueva is claimed by many, both within and outside the municipio, to be corrupt and inefficient. Furthermore, the municipio is a land of relic haciendas that became ejidos in the early 1930s. Near Tayahua in the far south, the 100,000-acre estate of Jesus Aguilar (the father of Mexican singer and movie star Antonio Aguilar) has been partitioned into ejidos; the same is true of Malpaso's fortresslike 25,000-acre hacienda in the far north. However, the residual estates, still privately owned, are much better than the ejido land—much of it hilly, isolated, and suitable only for grazing. Unlike Luis Moya, the municipio sends a large number of its fathers and sons to the United States to work, and some do not return. For this and other reasons, Villanueva's male-to-female ratio is low (table 2.1).

The municipio of Jerez is diversified, with commercial as well as subsistence agriculture and with urban trade and manufacturing befitting the third-largest city in the state (34,319 in 1990). Turning west from

Highway 54 south of Zacatecas and traversing a natural corridor through the mountains, after some 30 miles (48 km) one reaches the city of Jerez, at an elevation of 6,600 feet (2,011 m). Centered on the city, the municipio of Jerez has 58,000 people distributed over 600 square miles (1,556 km²). The land includes a rich floodplain, along which several reservoirs have been built, bordered to the east and west by spurs, 7,000 to 9,200 feet high (2,134–2,804 m), of the Sierra Madre Occidental. The landscape is gentle and tranquil, as idealized in the poetry of famous native son Ramón López Velarde (1888–1921), who is known for his patriotic poem *La Suave Patria*. Permanent streams, cool mountain air, and rich soils encouraged the Spanish to establish the villa of Jerez a hundred years before they settled Luis Moya or Villanueva. The area became the principal grain and meat supplier for the silver mines around Zacatecas and Fresnillo.

Today the area is noted for its peaches, which were started in the early 1970s with the benefit of remittances and knowledge gained from migrants who worked the peach orchards of California's Central Valley. In addition, apples, grapes, chiles, and alfalfa are grown, and many cattle are raised. The city of Jerez is a major retail and wholesale center that also produces beverages, wood products, and basic hardware goods. Despite this sophistication, as in Villanueva there are many small towns in the mountains that do not benefit from the commerce. Demographically, however, Jerez is more like Luis Moya than Villanueva. It has a relatively high income, moderate inequality, and a relatively high rate of manufacturing. However, like Villanueva, it is slow growing and has a high rate of migration to the United States.

The nearby city of Zacatecas is included for comparison and context. With a population of 100,051 (1990), it is one of the smallest state capitals. At 7,900 feet (2,408 m), it is surrounded (and underlain) by some of the richest silver deposits in the world. Its establishment in the mid-1500s began the colonial period of mining, ranching, and agriculture in the state. The city is the regional growth center for business and repair services, higher-order medical and educational services, fine shopping goods, entertainment, and (along with Fresnillo and Calera) manufacturing. It is itself tributary to larger cities such as Aguascalientes and San Luis Potosí. Its demographic profile reflects a surplus of females, high population growth, high income, and relatively low inequality of income (table 2.1). Despite the figure in the table, the U.S. migration rate for Zacatecas is much lower than for the other municipios (see note d, table 2.1).

Northern Coahuila

Northern Coahuila lies just east of the Sierra Madre Oriental (fig. 2.1) between Piedras Negras and Monclova on the Gulf Coastal Plain. It varies from 500 feet (152 m) elevation at the eastern border of the state along the Río Grande (Río Bravo), to 750 feet (229 m) at Piedras Negras and 2,000 feet (610 m) at Monclova. Thus, the region is a tilted table oriented like the Mesa del Norte itself in miniature. Three important rivers flow eastward across the region into the Río Bravo—the Escondido, the Sabinas, and the Salado (fig. 2.3). At the confluence of the Sabinas and the Salado, near the boundary with Nuevo León, lies the Venustiano Carranza reservoir; above Villa Acuña lies the Amistad Reservoir on the Río Bravo itself. Coupled with the fertile soils in these basins, and the springs in the rivers' upper courses, these reservoirs stimulate agricultural development in the region. The current economic base also owes much to the region's geology. At the end of the Cretaceous period (70 million years ago), the Gulf of Mexico covered the region to the base of the Sierra Madres. Then, active vulcanism coupled with uplift and faulting brought deposits of iron and dolomite to the surface in the south, around Monclova. During Tertiary times (70 million to 2 million years ago), as the sea retreated toward the current coastline, deep deposits of coal and lignite were formed from compressed marsh vegetation in coastal lagoons. This is the Sabinas Basin coal field around Nueva Rosita and Sabinas—the largest coal deposit in the country. Finally, in Quaternary times (the last 2 million years), rivers have deposited their fertile sediments southward across the Gulf Coastal Plain, including the whole area southeastward from Morelos and Allende.

The climate of the region is subtropical steppe (BS in Köppen) with the exception of the area from Nueva Rosita to Morelos, which, owing to somewhat higher rainfall, is considered humid subtropical (Cfa). Although rainfall on the plain itself is low—around 14 inches (36 cm) at both Monclova and Sabinas—the mountains west of Nueva Rosita and Monclova receive twice that, owing to the orographic effect of the Sierras receiving moisture-laden Gulf air from the east. Rainfall is concentrated in the summer half of the year; September, on average, is the wettest month (due to tropical storms), and the late spring is also wet. In the summer, the area is an *"horno"* (furnace), with temperatures above 110 degrees Fahrenheit (43° C) some days. Vegetation reflects this climate. Northern Coahuila, much like its counterpart region across the Río Grande (the south Texas Brush Country), supports a native cover of mesquite and cactus (sotol,

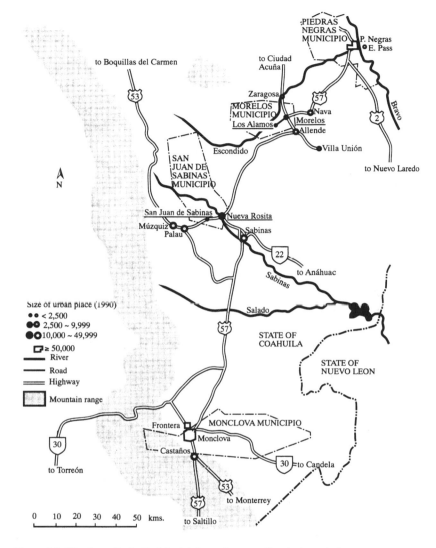

Figure 2.3 Northern Coahuila: Municipios and towns of study (sampled towns are underlined)

lechuguilla, nopal, biznaga, organ pipe, dagger yucca). However, where ground or surface water exists, the area blooms with tropical vegetables, fruits, and pasturage for commercial dairy and beef operations.

As in the case of south-central Zacatecas, the physical environment of northern Coahuila does not offer a complete explanation for the region's large-scale migration to the United States. Here, too, historical and political factors are important.

Historical Forces

Northern Coahuila is an extension, physically, of the Brush Country of south Texas, and shares both its prehistory and its colonial history. The same Amerindians roamed both areas, and both areas were governed by Spain during the colonial period. The Indians that the Spanish found in the region—the Coahuiltecans—were among the most primitive in North America. They may have been forced into an area not coveted by the more advanced Athabaskan groups which pushed down the Rockies and Sierra Madres into central Mexico. The Coahuiltecans were primitive hunters and gatherers, roving from place to place, eating everything in their environment that the human organism could digest (Newcomb 1961, 29–57). Their legacy is important, nonetheless. The Coahuiltecans ate the pods of the mesquite tree and the buds and pulp of the nopal and sotol; they drank peyote tea and mezcal. Today, peasant families of the region follow the same practices. The Coahuiltecans harvested ixtle (lechuguilla and palma) cacti for their coarse fibers, which they wove into shoes; today, ixtle gathering is practiced throughout Coahuila, Zacatecas, and San Luis Potosí—a fallback activity when crops fail, urban jobs are scarce, or U.S. migration is difficult.

During the early colonial period, northern Coahuila, known as Nueva Extremadura, was the focus of a cluster of Franciscan missions designed to protect the wealthier settlements to the south and to "reduce," or civilize, the Indians of the region. After the establishment of settlements at Saltillo and Monclova in the late 1500s, in 1674 a line of missions to the north—Candela, Múzquiz, Sabinas, and Villa Unión—was established. All were abandoned shortly afterward. Adding to the pressures due to the tremendous differences in Spanish and Indian lifestyles, the *encomenderos* (noble recipients of land from the Spanish Crown) insisted on capturing and enslaving the natives. Later (around 1700), four missions were founded along the Río Grande at Guerrero, 30 miles south of present-day Piedras Negras. These were more successful. Grain fields were irrigated by means of an aqueduct linking Guerrero with springs in the Morelos area, 60 miles to the west (Villarello Vélez 1969, 67–91). Thus, even then the fertile plains and water of the region were used to benefit the inhabitants. The Crown continued to grant large land parcels to encomenderos, and one—the Marques de Aguayo—until independence owned 14 million acres in parcels that stretched from south of Saltillo to Monclova, a distance of over 200 miles. Most of the encomendero land had been sold by 1821 but remained in large parcels. These became the basis for the ranching economy of the subsequent one hundred years.

Economically, independence scarcely affected northern Coahuila or northern Mexico in general. Although in 1810 Father Hidalgo marched north and "took" Saltillo, Coahuila was a criollo state that, like its neighbors, supported independence but not social revolution. Hidalgo's reduced army was captured, and after imprisonment in Monclova, he and his principal general, Ignacio Allende, were sent to Chihuahua and executed (Fehrenbach 1973, 331–32). Ironically (in light of later history), Allende had intended to seek support in Texas in return for agreement to support Texas's claim to independent nationhood. After independence, the conservative society continued essentially unchanged under the Mexican flag. Northeastern Coahuila was a land of cattle, grain, and cotton haciendas, and these prospered under the Porfiriato. In addition, the building of the Piedras Negras–Saltillo railroad in 1894 and the establishment of the HYLSA steel plant in 1903 in Monterrey (which stimulated coal mining in Sabinas Basin) generated substantial employment for the region (Cardoso 1980, 13–17; Jones 1984). Northeastern Coahuila became, in turn, a funnel through which many central Mexicans crossed the border to work on the ranches and the vegetable, melon, beet, and citrus farms of Texas and nearby U.S. states (Taylor 1930, 295–307; Cardoso 1980, 13–19) and to construct the Atchison, Topeka, Santa Fe, and Missouri Pacific railroads across Texas (Corwin 1978, 31–61; Jones 1984).

The Mexican Revolution was a time of fire and blood, in which over a million lost their lives out of a 1910 Mexican population of 15 million (by contrast, 620,000 died in the U.S. Civil War, of an 1860 population of 31 million). Ironically, although the cradle of revolution was in the north (Francisco I. Madero and Venustiano Carranza were from Coahuila; Pancho Villa was from Chihuahua), the battles were fought on the plains and mountains of central and southern Mexico. But northern Coahuila did not fully escape the political terror. In 1912, 1913, and 1916 the populations of Villa Acuña and Piedras Negras fled across the U.S. border from attacks by Villistas. Communities of Coahuilan families became established in San Antonio, Brownsville, and Laredo at that time (Cardoso 1980, 40). However, Villa's main focus was the Terrazas family's economic interests in Chihuahua, and thus Coahuila was less affected economically.

Postrevolutionary Coahuila recovered relatively quickly, providing jobs in mining, manufacturing, and agriculture for internal migrants streaming northward from the interior. In the fierce competition for jobs, many native Coahuilans were displaced by the flood of migrants from the north-central region. Texas attracted many of these displaced migrants—to new irrigated agriculture in both the High Plains and the Lower Valley, and to urban jobs in cities such as San Antonio, where in 1928, for example, people of Mexican origin made up 81 percent of the manufacturing work force (Benke 1982, 30).

Since 1940, northern Coahuila has shared in the growth that has characterized peripheral Mexico. Much of this growth has been connected with public works and manufacturing. Significant events of the period include the establishment of Altos Hornos de México, the steel plant in Monclova, in 1941; the construction of the Amistad Dam in 1963; and the building of the Nava thermoelectric plant in 1969, all of which illustrate the dynamic nature of the region.

The Economy Today

Northern Coahuila's mining and agricultural sectors today account for only 10 to 15 percent of total employment (compared to one-half in Zacatecas). This leaves 85 to 90 percent of the workers in the region employed in manufacturing, construction, retail, wholesale, and service activities. The Altos Hornos integrated steel plant opened in Monclova in 1941. The plant has had a tremendous impact on employment in the Sabinas Basin (including Nueva Rosita and Sabinas; see fig. 2.3), its major source of coal. In addition, the Hercules iron mine, west of Múzquiz at the Chihuahua border, and the huge Chrysler and General Motors automobile plants at Ramos Arizpe near Saltillo, have backward and forward linkages (respectively) with the Monclova plant, generating thousands of jobs. The Sabinas Basin has also attracted coke plants, a zinc plant (at Nueva Rosita), and a thermoelectric plant (at Nava, near Morelos), which hire thousands. Maquiladoras have opened up new employment opportunities since their establishment in the region over the last decade. In 1989, Piedras Negras and Ciudad Acuña had a combined total of almost 21,000 maquila workers in 58 plants (McCray 1989, 10). Because these plants pay several times the minimum wage in Mexico, and because they employ workers from interior towns such as Morelos and Allende (who commute by company buses to their jobs), they support a large number of retail and service activities in the region. Finally, the region has important dairy and beef cattle farms, grain farms, and pecan orchards, which in turn support such factories as dairies and flour mills.

Rather than suffering from political forces (as southern Zacatecas has), northern Coahuila has benefited from them. The location of the AHMSA (Altos Hornos de México, S.A.) steel plant in Monclova was a decision overseen by the government. The maquiladoras are along the U.S. border because of special Mexican policies encouraging them to locate there. The Mexican government's current support for the elimination of import tariffs—part of the free trade accord with the United States—will make the region very attractive for raising winter garden fruits and vegetables for U.S. grocery chains. In addition, both U.S. and Mexican agribusinesses might decide to locate fruit and vegetable processing plants in the region because of its proximity to large markets in San Antonio, Houston, and Dallas.

A demographic and economic profile of northern Coahuila (table 2.2) shows that it is more urbanized and somewhat better off economically, although much slower growing, than the country as a whole. Almost nine out of ten people live in urban areas; manufacturing employs more workers than agriculture; monthly income is above the national average; and income inequalities are below the national average. Population growth is low as a result of declines in mining and manufacturing in the Nueva Rosita area during the 1970s and 1980s. U.S. migration rates are quite high, due to two factors: more family ties in the United States, stemming from past migration and regularization of status; and the transfer of migrants to the United States in a stepwise migration process from the north-central region to the north and then to the United States.

The Study Municipios

The two municipios chosen for study, Morelos and San Juan de Sabinas, are illustrative of the differences across the northern Coahuila region. As with Zacatecas, I will also briefly discuss the metropolitan municipios of the region—in this case Monclova and Piedras Negras—which are excluded from the migration and impact analyses of chapters 3 through 6. The latter two further illustrate the variety within the region and offer a comparison with the nonmetropolitan municipios.

The municipio of Morelos is found in the northeastern part of the state of Coahuila, only 33 miles (53 km) by Route 57 from the metropolitan

Table 2.2 Selected Socioeconomic Indicators: Mexico and Northern Coahuila, 1990

Indicator	Mexico	Study Municipios in Northern Coahuila			Piedras Negras mcpo. (for comparison)	Monclova mcpo. (for comparison)
		Total, 2 mcpos	Morelos	S. Juan Sabinas		
Population (thousands)	81,250	46.9	6.6	40.2	98.2	178.6
Population growth, 1970–1980 (%)	21.5	8.7	10.7	8.4	22.3	49.3
Sex ratio (males per 100 females)	96.5	96.7	98.6	96.2	97.0	100.0
% urban (places of 5,000+ pop.)	65.6	89.2	83.2	90.2	98.0	99.5
% labor force in agriculture	23.5	9.1	26.6	6.1	3.5	1.6
% labor force in manufacturing	19.9	10.9	15.9	10.1	30.9	37.6
Median monthly income (1990 pesos, thousands)	416	449	456	448	494	557
Median monthly income (1990 U.S. dollars)[a]	154	166	169	166	183	206
Inequality of income[b]	1.067	0.834	0.851	0.830	1.021	0.946
No. of migrants per 1,000 residents[c]	2.8	31.3	50.7	28.2	12.6	3.4

Source: *X Censo General de Población y Vivienda*, 1990, unless otherwise indicated.

a. Converted at a rate of 2,700 pesos to the dollar (mid-1990).

b. Standardized quartile deviation, defined as $(Q_3 - Q_1) / Md$, where Q_3, Q_1 = third and first income quartiles, respectively, and Md is the median.

c. Based on Immigration and Naturalization Service I-213 forms. Based on 1980 populations (Jones 1988).

area of Piedras Negras (population 96,178 in 1990) on the U.S. border (fig. 2.3). The town of Morelos, with 5,534 people (1990), holds 80 percent of the municipio's population—a not uncommon situation in dry northern Mexico, where population is aggregated at a few favorable locations such as at a spring or along a river, at a mine, or at an old political capital. In Morelos the attraction is the springs, which support a rich agricultural tradition with its roots in colonial times. The town, set among tall trees and canals, is green and tranquil. This is the area of *los cinco manatiales* (the five springs)—a sort of central oasis some twenty miles in diameter and centered on Allende, which encompasses the capitals of five municipios—Morelos, Zaragosa, Allende, Villa Unión, and Nava. The municipio boundaries radiate outward from these capitals as from the hub of a wheel. Fertile soils of the coastal plain and a humid subtropical climate support corn, sorghum, dairy cattle, beef cattle, pecans, and fruits; the surroundings are reminiscent of the Winter Garden area of south Texas.

By national standards, Morelos has below-average population growth and average income levels (table 2.2). In addition to U.S. migration, the Morelos economy benefits from out-commuting to nearby plants and from its own local manufacturing sector (in fact, 16 percent of the municipal labor force works in manufacturing, a very high figure for a municipio of 7,000 people; see table 2.2). Each day, company buses arrive to carry several hundred workers either to the apparel maquiladora in Piedras Negras, where pants are manufactured, or to the thermoelectric plant and the Micari lignite mine at Nava. Another 200 work at the Liconsa milk plant in Morelos. It may be surmised that in Morelos, a family considering U.S. migration has two or three other serious options. The municipio's very high rate of U.S. migration, based on estimates in Jones (1988), may be somewhat overstated due to the idiosyncrasies in the sample employed in that study. However, the municipio clearly does have many U.S. migrants, based on findings from the present study. This migration is due to its proximity to Texas, the long-standing family ties there, and the relative ease of getting legal papers to cross the border.

The municipio of San Juan de Sabinas is as different from Morelos as night from day. Superficially similar to Morelos in terms of its urbanization rate, manufacturing level, and income level (see table 2.2), San Juan de Sabinas is an area of heavy industry and mining. Nueva Rosita (36,284 people in 1990), the county seat, is located on Highway 57 midway along the 150-mile (242 km) strip between Piedras Negras and Monclova. It is a city set among slag heaps and smokestacks, and is stark, grey, and polluted.

Nueva Rosita is situated on a tributary of the Sabinas River, in a humid subtropical area east of the Sierra Madres Orientales, which loom in the distance. Rainfall (around 24 inches per year) as well as springs support wheat and corn cultivation on ejidos in the northern part of the municipio. But the history of Rosita (as the town is known popularly) is mainly tied to mining—in particular the opening of two steel mills, one in Monterrey in 1903 and another in Monclova in 1941. Rosita sits astraddle the Sabinas coal basin, the largest reserve of metallurgical bituminous coal in the country and the main supplier of coking coal for the two steel complexes. Workers from Rosita commute to the strip mines and coke plants that dot the landscape. In addition, until recently more than 1,200 people worked at a large zinc-ore reduction plant (IMMSA, or Industria Minera de México, S.A., formerly ASARCO, the U.S. transnational) in Rosita itself. The plant was a notorious polluter, creating horrendous grey ash storms that covered whole colonias in its vicinity. (Not surprisingly, one of the largest lung hospitals is located in Rosita, supported in part from mine workers' salaries). After cutbacks, the IMMSA plant was finally closed in 1985. Coupled with the decline of the local coal industry, in part due to competition from imported coal, the closing of the zinc smelter dealt a severe blow to the economy of Rosita. U.S. migration, facilitated by extensive family ties, became a more important option for the people here.

Even more than San Juan de Sabinas, Monclova (which is outside the study area, but included for comparison) illustrates the role of heavy industry in the economy of northern Coahuila. Monclova owes its current prosperity to a decision more than 50 years ago by ARMCO Steel and the Mexican government to locate a steel mill there. AHMSA (Altos Hornos de México, S.A.) soon became the largest integrated steel mill in Latin America. Illustrating industrial location theory in action, this decision was based on Monclova's low total transport costs for the iron ore (from Chihuahua and Durango), coking coal (from the Sabinas Basin), and limestone (from the dolomite-rich mountains south of Monclova itself). Proximity to the United States market was also a factor. The city (population 177,792 in 1990, with nearby Ciudad Frontera adding another 58,000) is strategically located 120 miles (193 km) north of Coahuila and 150 miles (242 km) south of the U.S. border on Route 57, at 2,000 feet (610 m) in the foothills of the Sierra Madres Orientales.

AHMSA transformed the city from an agricultural and textile town of 9,000 in 1940 to the third-largest city in Coahuila today (after Torreon and Saltillo). In 1990, the 24,000 persons hired by AHMSA accounted for

48 percent of the city's entire labor force. The city also has many linked manufacturing plants, producing tanks, pipes, and parts, in addition to a large retail service area, making it the "growth pole of central Coahuila." Its public service sector is also dynamic, with modern schools, hospitals, streets, and museums; many of these were projects of the eminent Harold Pape, the ARMCO representative who spearheaded AHMSA's locational decision and, with his wife, Lou, donated millions to social projects in their adopted hometown. Monclova has its problems—the decline of AHMSA in the period 1971–86, pollution, a diminishing water supply—but its growth and its social and economic health have transcended these problems. Monclova is an employment pole for central Coahuila; it sends relatively few migrants to the United States.

Piedras Negras municipio (also included for comparison) is dominated by the city of Piedras Negras, a metropolitan area of some 96,000 in 1990, the fourth largest in the state. Piedras, situated at 750 feet (229 m) elevation on the Río Bravo, on the Gulf Coastal Plain, is more independent of its physical environment than the other cities of northern Coahuila. A very fast-growing area, the municipio grew by 72 percent over the 1970s but slowed to 22 percent by the 1980s. This growth has been due to two principal factors—border trade and maquiladora industrialization. Maquila employment in 1989 was over 7,400—almost one-quarter of the total labor force in Piedras. In addition, the city has a small steel mill, tied to AHMSA in Monclova. As a port of entry, Piedras has a thriving retail sector that serves Mexican shoppers from the interior and U.S. tourists crossing the border in both directions. In addition, tourism from the large Amistad Reservoir to the north benefits the city. Owing to its strategic entrepot position, Piedras Negras is the origin for many migrants to the United States.

Conclusions

The history, politics, and physical environments of the two study areas lie just beneath the surface of events, helping to explain the current economy as well as migration behavior. Central Zacatecas, with median incomes considerably below the national average, has had a difficult history. During the independence and revolutionary periods, the region was ravaged by opposing armies. In between, haciendas controlled much of the land and labor. The postrevolutionary period has been a time of continuing political conflict and failed agricultural institutions and policies. Bad weather and the decline of world silver prices have added to the generally negative picture. U.S. migration established itself in the 1890s and accelerated with the revolution, the bracero epoch, and the economic collapse of the 1970s and 1980s.

Northern Coahuila, with incomes just above the national mean, has faced milder historical and political shocks, but has a high U.S. migration rate nonetheless. Its peripheral position with respect to the major struggles meant that independence and revolution, and the postrevolutionary rebellions, brought only temporary setbacks. The postrevolutionary period has brought certain favorable political trends, among them the establishment of more efficient collective ejidos, the building of large reservoirs and power plants, the location of the steel plant at Monclova, and the creation of the Border Industrialization Program. The level of U.S. migration from northern Coahuila owes more to migration networks created during the revolution, to proximity, and to the legalized status of many migrants, than to poor economic conditions. In both subregions the cultural forces—historical, political, economic—have been more important than the physical forces in accounting for U.S. migration.

3
Household Migration in Space and Time

As we have seen, Central Zacatecas has the profile of a backward, peripheral region that has been largely bypassed by the Mexican development miracle. Its economic profile—dryland agriculture, metallic mining, and cattle grazing—fits a bygone era. Northern Coahuila, while perhaps no less dependent on outside forces, is much more in the mainstream of current development initiatives in energy, commercial agriculture, and maquiladora manufacturing. Both regions, however, have high migration rates to the United States.

This chapter examines demographic and migration history data for households interviewed in nonmetropolitan central Zacatecas and northern Coahuila. The data were obtained from responses to questions in sections A (Datos demográficos de la casa) and C (Historia de la migración) of the household questionnaire (see appendix B). Information on all migrating household members was requested. To shorten the questionnaire, detailed data were collected only on the initial and most recent work trips to the United States, although the total number of trips and total time spent working in the United States were recorded for each household member. These data provide a fairly comprehensive picture of the extent and causes of migration in the two study regions.

Central Zacatecas

Zacatecas, of all the Mexican states, is commonly acknowledged to have the highest rate of U.S. migration. It lies at the periphery of the traditional migration hearth of west-central Mexico. Before analyzing the impacts of migration on the three study municipios—the topic of the next chapter—it is valuable to examine the extent of the migration as well as some of the factors that determine why some families go and some stay behind. The analyses in this section are derived from two separate data sets: a household data set, consisting of 596 cases; and an individual migrant data set, consisting of 710 cases.

Temporal Trends

Migration from Zacatecas, as measured by initial work trips, follows a roller-coaster pattern superimposed on a generally rising trend (fig. 3.1). It shows a general rise through the early 1950s, a slight dip over the subsequent decade, a strong increase from the late 1960s through the late 1970s, another dip in the early 1980s, and a surge in the late 1980s. The dip during the 1950s came at the time of massive deportations by the U.S. Immigration and Naturalization Service (INS)—an initiative known as "Operation Wetback." This was also a time when the economic situation in Mexico was improving: in 1958, Mexico ended three consecutive six-year conservative administrations (Camacho, Alemán, and Cortines) that promoted extensive public works, foreign investment, and economic development. Although they targeted the cities, such policies had a trickle-down effect on rural regions like Zacatecas. In the late 1960s, U.S. migration picked up markedly. This was the time of development without trickle-down, under the authoritarian regime of Díaz Ordaz (1964–70);

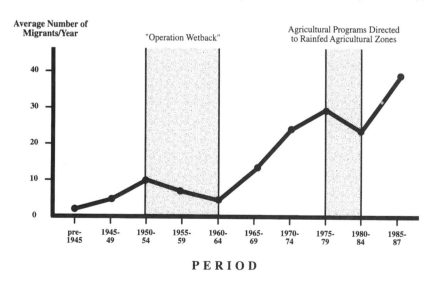

Figure 3.1 Central Zacatecas: Annual number of first-time migrants to the United States

the resulting deterioration of rural Mexico's economic situation continued into the Echeverría administration (1970–76).

The dip in the early 1980s marked the delayed effect of massive rural development schemes beginning with Echeverría and continuing under López Portillo (1976–82)—in the latter case, financed with government proceeds from the oil boom. Until the bottom fell out in 1982, the government was engaged in what López Portillo termed "managing prosperity." The development schemes included the SAM (the Sistema Alimentario Mexicano, or Mexican Food System), which subsidized corn and bean prices); and the PIDER (Programa de Inversiones Públicas para el Desarrollo Rural, or Program of Public Investment for Rural Development), which financed projects in rain-fed districts (Grindle 1988, 145–51). These programs targeted less-developed regions such as Zacatecas. Totally dependent on central government financing and planning, the programs collapsed when the oil crisis hit. By the late 1980s, economic crisis had come to the region, and out-migration from central Zacatecas rebounded with a vengeance. Out-migration was further propelled by a two-year drought in 1986–87, during which no corn or beans were harvested. These sample trends for central Zacatecas closely reflect those found in studies that present data for total emigration from Mexico to the United States (e.g., Cornelius 1978, 8–9; Simcox 1988).

Migrant Legal Status and Job Characteristics

In this section, three broad periods of U.S. migration are defined: before 1965; 1965 to 1979; and 1980 and afterward. Migrants from 1942 to 1964 were predominantly braceros—workers contracted by U.S. employers, overseen by the two federal governments. The time from 1965 to 1979 was a period of burgeoning, largely undocumented migration from rural regions of north-central and west-central Mexico. Most of this migration was stimulated as much by pull factors in the United States (jobs in a booming U.S. economy) as by push factors in Mexico (development without trickle-down and failed agricultural programs). The year 1980 marked another turning point. In the 1980s Mexico faced its most severe economic crisis since the revolution—the collapse of petroleum prices and with them the government's financial solvency; resultant capital flight; inflation and peso devaluation; and, cruelly, the most powerful earthquake to hit Mexico in thirty years. Migration in this period was mostly

Table 3.1 Migrant Characteristics by Year of First U.S. Work Trip: Central Zacatecas

	Pre-1965	1965–1979	1980 & after
Number of migrants in sample (n)[a]	134	324	252
% of migrants in sample	18.8	45.7	35.5
% male	95.5	81.4	87.6
Legal status			
% bracero	73.4	3.1	0
% illegal	13.3	80.7	93.2
% other	13.3	16.2	6.8
Total	100.0	100.0	100.0
U.S. job			
Rural (unskilled)	89.6	25.9	17.3
Unskilled urban	8.8	68.2	80.9
Skilled urban	1.6	5.9	1.8
Total	100.0	100.0	100.0
Destination			
California	45.0	70.4	76.6
Other, West	14.1	7.6	7.4
Texas	31.7	4.8	3.3
Other, South	2.5	.3	0
Illinois	4.2	15.5	11.7
Other, North-central	2.5	1.2	.4
Northeast	0	0	.4
Total	100.0	99.8	99.8

a. Total sample migrants by period; different variables have different numbers of missing cases. Total $n = 710$.

undocumented and was stimulated primarily by economic "push" factors in Mexico. The U.S. economy exerted little "pull," because it was in recession. (Nevertheless, the amnesty provisions of the 1986 Immigration Reform and Control Act did serve as a social pull factor.) During this period the sending regions in Mexico broadened to include urban areas as well as regions farther south that previously had experienced little U.S. migration.

The great majority of early (pre-1965), first-time Zacatecas migrants were braceros taking unskilled rural jobs in western agriculture (table 3.1, first column). At that time the western U.S. states grew a great deal of the country's cotton, citrus, winter vegetables, sugar beets, and apples (as they still do). In the early 1940s, wartime demand accelerated production of these crops, creating labor shortages which the growers convinced the U.S. government could be filled only with braceros. As noted in chapter 2, Zacatecas received high bracero quotas from the Mexican government.

Most beginning migrants after 1965 had to enter illegally due to the termination of the bracero program, but once across the border they were free to work at the job and in the place of their choosing (table 3.1, columns 2 and 3). There was a progressive trend toward California as the destination of choice after 1980, despite the greater proximity of Texas to Zacatecas (the city of Zacatecas is 420 miles, or 676 km, from the Texas border but 1,300 miles, or 2,093 km, from the California border). California is superior to Texas in wages, working conditions, and social milieu, and this offsets its remoteness. For example, wages for labor are higher there, illegal workers' rights are more respected, the U.S. Border Patrol uses less discriminatory tactics, and there are organized migrant social clubs. To the undocumented worker, California is the "promised land" (Jones 1984).

Migrants also showed an increasing preference for urban over rural work after 1965, which reflects both the decline in agricultural jobs and the attractiveness of less arduous work and urban amenities. The urban jobs were, nevertheless, largely unskilled. The unskilled urban jobs most commonly taken by migrants in our Zacatecas sample in the 1980s were (in order) restaurant work (busboy, dishwasher), menial factory work, work in bakeries and tortillerías, child care and housekeeping, construction, hotel and casino work, sewing, jobs as mechanics' assistants, gardening, and janitorial work. John Naisbitt has incisively pointed out that our high-tech society has created a parallel demand for "high-touch" jobs—those that are personalized, quality-of-life enhancing, and nonmechanizable (Naisbitt 1984, 35–52). Many of the above jobs fit the "high-touch" category— services that a wealthy and busy society demands but that its members don't want to perform themselves. Others are simply dirty, insecure, physically demanding jobs that no one else wants. Zacatecans, among the most destitute of Mexican migrants, fill these jobs—an irony that leads one to contemplate some of the fundamental inequities in the world and yet still conclude that the net result is positive on both sides of the border. Although it is not reflected in the table, for the individual migrant there is job mobility between first and latest jobs, regardless of period, in terms of movement from a rural to an urban unskilled job (see Jones and Murray 1986). However, movement from an unskilled to a skilled urban job is infrequent, because it usually entails direct competition with U.S. urban minorities.

Since 1980, the population of beginning migrants has become more predominantly male and illegal; and these people have tended to enter many more unskilled urban jobs, as opposed to either rural jobs or skilled urban jobs, than the migrants of the 1965–79 period. Coupled with the accelerated pace of migration (fig. 3.1), this paints a rather grim picture of the local economic opportunities for Mexican males living in the north-central region in the 1980s. The picture is one of new migrant sons and heads of household—forced into the migration stream by the economic crisis that afflicted all of Mexico—willing to risk illegal entry and willing to take whatever work was available. This representation is consistent with recent analysis of U.S. Immigration and Naturalization Service data for undocumented Mexican apprehensions in the San Antonio Border Patrol sector for the period 1987–92 (Jones 1994).

Migration Selectivity

The question of migration selectivity is how such demographic characteristics as sex, age, household size, education, occupation, marital status, rurality, and stage in the life cycle influence who migrates and who does not.

The household is defined as related persons customarily living in the same house. It includes the nuclear family, other relations (extended family) living in the house, and family members who are temporarily living elsewhere, for example, in the United States. It excludes family members who have moved away permanently, such as daughters or sons who have married and founded their own households. The household is the most important decision-making unit in Mexican society. Decisions made within the family include how many children to have and how to raise them, where to live, what to consume and invest in, what types of work to engage in, and whether and where to migrate in search of additional family income.

The migration experience measure used is the recency of U.S. migration, defined in terms of the year in which the head of household was most recently working in the United States. Three migrant types are identified: (1) active, defined as one who worked in the United States at some time within the three years prior to and including 1988 (when the interviews took place); (2) dormant, defined as one who worked in the United States, but not during the three years prior to 1988; and (3) nonmigrant, one who never worked in the United States. This measure is appropriate for analyzing relationships between migration and current demographic characteristics.

The results indicate that migration is a highly selective process in central Zacatecas (table 3.2). In comparison with nonmigrants, active migrant heads of household are more predominantly young and male. This suggests the arduousness of the journey into the United States, of the search for a job there, and of the work itself. Since 1985 these have all become

Table 3.2 Demographic Characteristics of Household Heads in Central Zacatecas (Migration Selectivity)

| Characteristic (Variable) | Nonmi-grant Household Heads | Migrant Household Heads | | All House-hold Heads |
		Dormant (latest U.S. work trip before 1985)	Active (latest U.S. work trip 1985 & after)	
Number of HH heads in sample (n)[a]	331	175	90	596
% of Sample HH heads	55.5	29.4	15.1	100.0
% male	87.6	97.1	96.7	91.8
Age				
34 and younger	22.4	16.6	47.8	24.5
35–50	39.0	38.3	41.1	39.1
50 and older	38.7	45.1	11.1	36.4
Total	100.1	100.0	100.0	100.0
Education				
Less than 3 years	39.6	33.7	23.3	35.4
3–5 years	29.6	42.3	46.7	35.9
6 years and more	30.8	24.0	30.0	28.7
Total	100.0	100.0	100.0	100.0
Occupation in Mexico				
Agriculture	42.8	64.4	69.2	53.2
Unskilled urban	37.1	25.0	23.1	31.4
Skilled urban	6.7	3.0	1.3	4.8
Professional/technical	13.4	7.3	6.4	10.5
Total	100.0	99.7	100.0	99.9
% Living in rural areas (< 5,000 pop.)	58.6	69.7	80.0	65.1
% Married[b]	83.5	92.4	97.8	88.2
Numbers of HH members				
fewer than 4	30.2	26.4	26.7	28.6
4–7	37.8	39.1	40.0	38.5
8 and more	32.0	34.5	33.3	32.9
Total	100.0	100.0	100.0	100.0
Stage of life cycle				
Single or married w/o children	7.1	4.5	2.2	5.6
All children < 13	24.9	25.9	48.3	28.7
Some children 13 & above	48.0	42.5	42.7	45.6
All children 13 & above	20.0	27.0	6.7	20.1
Total	100.0	99.9	99.9	100.0

a. Total households by migrant category. Different variables have different numbers of missing cases.
b. Including "free unions."

more difficult due to a combination of factors including increased crimi-
nality at the border, recession in the United States, and competition for
jobs among the flood of new migrants (Jones 1994). Migrants from Zacatecas, often trusting and fatalistic, must endure abuses from Mexican officials, coyotes, thieves, and worse. Coming from a traditional part of Mexico, unversed in how to act in order to avoid apprehension, they often hike
overland from the border to their places of employment, avoiding roads
and cities. Many do not have relatives at their intended destinations to in-
form them of job opportunities or to help them in landing a job, so they
must travel about, asking for work. These obstacles tend to cull out older
migrants and women.

Compared to nonmigrants, more active migrant heads of household
work in agriculture, and (surprisingly) they are better educated (table 3.2).
Their higher education is not so surprising when it is remembered that the
active migrants are much younger. They have obtained their education in
recent years, when Mexico has had more and better schools and teachers.
Interestingly, even though only 53 percent of all household heads in central Zacatecas worked in agriculture (in Mexico), 69 percent of active migrants did so. This is an indication of the current economic difficulties in
rural central Zacatecas, and in fact, in all of rural central Mexico. Those
sectors whose dynamism had begun to restore Mexico's trade balance in
the late 1980s—maquiladoras and other industry, tourism, and commercial agriculture—are largely absent from this region, and particularly from
the municipios with high rates of migration. Faced with inflation and unemployment, with no regional growth centers nearby to provide jobs,
many families perceive U.S. migration to be the only alternative. A small
professional and technical "elite" exists in central Zacatecas, but only a
small proportion of U.S. migrants come from that sector (table 3.2).

Heads of household who are active migrants tend to be married, and
their families are at an earlier point in the life cycle—that imaginary continuum from marriage to death—than those of nonmigrants (table 3.2).
The active migrant household has a profusion of young children, and this
suggests that providing for the needs and aspirations of a growing number
of dependents may exert an important influence on the head's decision to
work in the United States. The results of the life cycle classification in
table 3.2, suggested by Massey and his colleagues (1987), support the con-
tention that between early marriage (when a man wants to be at home with
his wife) and the late-nuclear stage (when the children are themselves old
enough to work), there is an intense period of U.S. migration targeted to

meeting family economic needs. Parenthetically, and sadly, this is also a formative period when children most need the guidance of a father.

The Study Municipios Compared

This section examines the variation in U.S. migration experience across the three survey municipios. These municipios differ in their degrees of urbanization, education, and commerciality and so may be expected to have different levels of participation in U.S. migration. To allow a comprehensive examination of the different dimensions of migration, I consider four distinct indicators: actuality, or whether anyone has ever worked in the United States; recency, defined in terms of when a household member most recently worked in the United States (the active, dormant, or nonmigrant classification); quantity, that is, the total number of months cumulated by all household members working in the United States; and frequency, the total number of work trips to the United States cumulated by household members.

The high level of U.S. migration, regardless of municipio, supports all that has been written about Zacatecas (table 3.3). Between 54 and 79 percent of central Zacatecas households had participated in U.S. migration, depending on the municipio. On average, more than two-thirds of all households in our sample had a U.S. migrant at some point, and approximately one-third either had an active migrant, had at least five years of cumulated migration experience, or had four or more work trips to the United States. These figures may seem high, but they are squarely in the middle of rates calculated for such west-central towns as Chamitlán, Michoacán, and Altamira, Jalisco (Massey et al. 1987, 112); Gómez Farías, Michoacán (López Castro 1986, 85); "Guadalupe," Michoacán (Reichert and Massey 1979); and Huecorio and Ihuatzio, Michoacán (Dinerman 1982, 41). This suggests that central Zacatecas shares its high U.S. migration rate with villages more solidly in the "migration hearth" of west-central Mexico. Many households began migrating before 1965. The bracero program may have given them a risk-free sample of U.S. life that motivated their migration (as undocumenteds) in later periods.

Despite the region's intensive involvement in U.S. migration, very few households were involved in migration to other Mexican cities and states. In this sense as well, central Zacatecas is similar to other states and towns of central Mexico (Shadow 1979; Zazueta and Corona 1979). By way of contrast, farther north in Cedral, San Luis Potosí, internal migration is

Table 3.3 Migration Comparisons for Municipios in Central Zacatecas

	Luis Moya (commercial agriculture)	Villanueva (subsistence agriculture)	Jerez (diversi- fied)	Total (all 3 mcpos.)
Migration Experience, All Households				
Number of households in sample (n)	102	302	192	596
% of HHs with U.S. migration experience[a]	53.9	68.2	79.2	69.3
% of HHs with active U.S. migrant[b]	30.4	32.5	54.2	39.1
% of HHs with ≥ 5 yrs. of U.S. migration[c]	18.6	31.5	42.7	32.9
% of HHs with ≥ 4 work trips to U.S.[d]	20.6	32.1	39.1	32.4
% of migrant HHs with first trip before 1965	39.0	29.8	37.7	33.7
% of migrant HHs with all undocumented[e]	58.5	79.5	69.1	72.9
% of all HHs with active Mexi- can (internal) migrant	11.8	14.6	6.3	11.4
Demographic Characteristics of Migrant versus Nonmigrant Households (Selectivity Analyses)				
Active migrant households:				
% of heads 34 years old and younger	50.0	48.6	46.3	47.8
% of heads with 3 yrs. education & more	66.7	78.4	77.8	76.7
% of heads who work in agriculture	70.0	71.9	66.7	69.2
% of heads who are rural	100.0	89.2	65.9	80.0
% of HHs with 8 members and more	41.7	40.5	24.4	33.3
% of HHs with all children < 13	25.0	50.0	53.7	48.3
Nonmigrant households:				
% of heads 34 years old and younger	29.0	21.7	18.3	22.4
% of heads with 3 yrs. education & more	48.4	63.1	63.4	60.4
% of heads who work in agriculture	48.3	43.6	35.0	42.8
% of heads who are rural	100.0	53.5	36.6	58.6
% of HHs with 8 members and more	33.9	33.3	26.8	32.0
% of HHs with all children <13	25.0	25.6	22.9	24.9
Migrant percentage minus non- migrant percentage:				
% of heads 34 years old and younger	21.0	26.9	28.0	25.4
% of heads with 3 yrs. education & more	18.3	15.3	14.4	16.3
% of heads who work in agriculture	21.7	28.3	31.7	26.4

Table 3.3 (*continued*)

	Luis Moya (commercial agriculture)	Villanueva (subsistence agriculture)	Jerez (diversi-fied)	Total (all 3 mcpos.)
Demographic Characteristics of Migrant versus Nonmigrant Households (Selectivity Analyses)				
Migrant percentage minus non-migrant percentage (continued):				
% of heads who are rural	0.0	35.7	29.3	21.4
% of HHs with 8 members and more	7.8	7.2	−2.4	1.3
% of HHs with all children <13	0.0	24.4	30.8	23.4
SELECTIVITY INDEX(ES)[f]	.108	.222	.254	.191

a. "Actuality"
b. "Recency
c. "Quantity"
d. "Frequency"
e. on latest trip; includes only migrants with at least one U.S. trip.
f. $\Sigma i; |\ M_i - N_i\ | / \Sigma_i |\ M_i + N_i\ |$, where M_i = the % figure for migrant households on se-lectivity characteristic i; and N_i = the % figure for nonmigrant households on selectivity

several times as prevalent as U.S. migration (Jones and Alvírez 1994). Apparently, Mexican families tend to practice either an international or an internal migration strategy, but not both.

Paradoxically, Jerez municipio, the most urbanized and economically diversified of the three municipios, has the greatest participation in U.S. migration. Villanueva municipio, a largely rural subsistence agricultural area, is next. The lowest participation rate is found in the commercial agricultural municipio of Luis Moya (table 3.3). The paradox of Jerez can be explained by the fact that its U.S. migration is not motivated by economic stagnation and the absence of alternatives, as it is in Villanueva. Migration from Jerez is impelled by migrant schemes for reinvestment back home—in commercial agriculture in the rural parts of the municipio and in family businesses in the city of Jerez. In 1988 an enthusiastic symbiosis between migration and investment existed in Jerez, where migrants returning from California were applying their learning and pouring their earnings into land, peach seedlings, agricultural machinery, and family businesses, as well as community projects and various consumer goods. This whole process was stimulated by the state governor, Genaro Borrego, who made it his policy to promote such linkages between migrant communities in southern California and their municipios of origin in Zacatecas. Thus, migration was not the effect of economic conditions; rather, it was the cause. Whether these investments will stimulate economic development and lessen future migration (Borrego's goal) is yet to be seen. Case studies of migration and reinvestment in Jerez are discussed at length in chapter 6.

With respect to selectivity, the three municipios reveal similar patterns (bottom three panels of table 3.3). In all three municipios, active migrant heads of household are younger, more educated, more rural, and more likely to be employed in agriculture than nonmigrant heads. In two out of the three municipios, active migrant households are larger and have more young children than nonmigrant households. Thus, the same type of selectivity is evident for each of the municipios. The differences are in the degree of selectivity. This can be measured by means of a selectivity index based on the absolute differences between the active migrant and nonmigrant percentages for each variable (see note f, table 3.3). The results (bottom panel, table 3.3) indicate that selectivity is most pronounced for Jerez and Villanueva, and least for Luis Moya.

This finding makes considerable sense. Previous studies (discussed in chapter 1) have concluded that in villages with longer U.S. migration histories and higher levels of U.S. migration, further migration increases socioeconomic inequalities within the village, in that a broadening base of long-term migrants finds itself increasingly removed from the nonmigrant class. This is tantamount to saying that migration will, over time, tend to select those families that have already cumulated U.S. migration experience. Jerez and Villanueva, with their higher levels of U.S. migration, would thereby be expected to exhibit more selectivity than Luis Moya. Furthermore, Luis Moya has more longstanding economic opportunities, a more dynamic economy, and greater income homogeneity (see table 2.1) than the other two municipios. For households in Luis Moya, U.S. migration is a less compelling option; there are, for example, opportunities for farmers in its commercial agricultural sector, and for more educated young people, in its apparel plants. Thus, migration does not select as strongly from these demographic groups in Luis Moya as in Villanueva or Jerez.

Northern Coahuila

Coahuila is located far from the Mexican migration hearth, but is so close to the United States that migration is pronounced despite the relative prosperity of the state. Family ties across the border have made it easier to obtain legal permits to cross and have facilitated the job search for residents of northern Coahuila. Again, two data sets form the basis for the analyses:

a household data set, consisting of 460 cases; and an individual migrant data set, consisting of 288 cases.

Temporal Trends

Migration from Coahuila exhibits the same pattern of increase as does migration from Zacatecas. There has been a general increase broken by two dips—one before 1965, the other between 1965 and 1980 (fig. 3.2). The first dip occurred in the late 1950s in response to the INS's "Operation Wetback" and to the improving economic conditions in Mexico. The second dip occurred in the early 1970s (a decade before the decline in migration from Zacatecas) and was related to the sudden increase in jobs in northern Coahuila during a period of rapid expansion of the steel industry in Monclova and Monterrey, for which northern Coahuila provides such inputs as coal, coke, and zinc. During this time, a large zinc plant at Nueva Rosita and coal mines near Morelos provided inputs for Monclova and Monterrey steel, while a thermoelectric plant at Nava (also near Morelos) provided energy for these and other industries. In the late 1970s, the upward trend in migration continued and accelerated, as more nationalistic administrations placed restrictions on the steel industry that curtailed efficiency, production, and jobs.

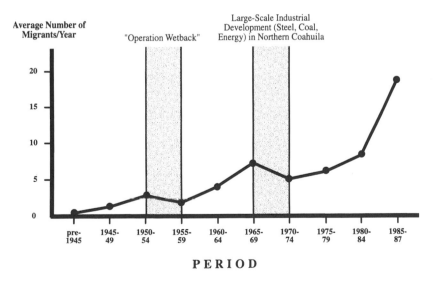

Figure 3.2 Northern Coahuila: Annual number of first-time migrants to the United States

The migration curve for Coahuila is smoother than that for Zacatecas—its hills and valleys less steep—suggesting that the changes in underlying physical, economic, and political forces have been less abrupt there. It is true that Coahuila's diversified economy and stronger legal migration profile has helped it smooth out the employment impacts of these fluctuations. Zacatecas has been more vulnerable to both Mexican economic policy and U.S. immigration policy; in addition, its dryland agriculture has been susceptible to periods of extended drought that have had much less effect on Coahuila, where agriculture tends to be irrigated.

Migrant Legal Status and Job Characteristics

Considering the same three broad periods as before, we see that, in Coahuila, proximity to the U.S. border played a decisive role in how migrants crossed, where they went, and what jobs they took (table 3.4). During the bracero epoch, Coahuila sent few workers. This reflects the fact that bra-

Table 3.4 Migrant Characteristics by Year of First U.S. Work Trip: Northern Coahuila

	Pre-1965	1965–1979	1980 & after
Number of migrants in sample (n)[a]	61	117	110
% of migrants in sample	21.2	40.6	38.2
% male	91.8	76.1	89.9
Legal status			
% bracero	15.1	0.9	0.0
% illegal	58.3	65.8	69.9
% other	26.4	33.3	30.1
Total	99.8	100.0	100.0
U.S. job			
Rural (unskilled)	66.0	43.8	22.1
Unskilled urban	20.8	46.7	58.9
Skilled urban	13.2	9.5	18.9
Total	100.0	100.0	99.9
Destination			
California	9.4	2.7	2.0
Other, West	0.0	4.5	2.0
Texas	83.0	71.2	86.3
Other, South	0.0	0.0	3.0
Illinois	5.7	17.1	6.9
Other, North-central	0.0	4.5	0.0
Northeast	1.9	0.0	0.0
Total	100.0	100.0	100.2

a. Total sample migrants by period; different variables have different numbers of missing cases. Total $n = 288$.

cero quotas for northern Mexico, set by the Mexican government, were very low (Cross and Sandos 1981, 35); in fact, Coahuila had no bracero recruiting centers (Chihuahua City to the west and Monterrey to the east were the closest; Jones 1984). In this period, migrants from Coahuila crossed either illegally or using temporary visas, and most went to Texas. These visas (the "other" category in table 3.4) included not only work permits and residency papers but also visitor cards with which the holder was not authorized to work; at least one-fourth of migrants used them (and use them today) to work.

By whatever method they crossed the border, migrants capitalized on long-standing family ties in the United States that helped them obtain legal documents (travel visas, work permits, and residency papers). Two-thirds worked in agriculture, because during the bracero period the greatest demand in Texas was for field hands. What is surprising is that one-third went into urban jobs (compared to just one-tenth for Zacatecas migrants during the same period). Of course, more Coahuilans came from urban areas in the first place; they also had ties to kin in Texas cities.

These trends continued after 1965, with one noteworthy exception: occupational mobility. Many more migrants now worked in urban jobs—almost four-fifths by the latest period (table 3.4), including nearly one-fifth in skilled urban jobs (compared to only 2 percent of Zacatecas migrants). The skilled jobs included carpenter, solderer, chauffeur, metalworker, and mason. This is where the superior education and urban origins of the Coahuilans really come into play. Nevertheless, a ceiling on continuing upward mobility within U.S. cities exists for Coahuilans as it does for Zacatecans; for every Coahuilan working in one of these skilled jobs, there were three working in unskilled jobs—for example, as construction laborers, gardeners, house cleaners or office janitors.

Migration Selectivity

Considering as we did for Zacatecas the relationship between a household's recency of U.S. migration and its demographic characteristics, we may conclude that migration is also a selective process in Coahuila (table 3.5). Migrants tended to be young and male to about the same degree as in Zacatecas. This may seem surprising given that the barriers for older migrants and women are not as great for the Coahuilans, with their transborder ties and legal status. However, consider two facts. First, there are many more opportunities for women in urbanized, industrialized

Table 3.5 Demographic Characteristics of Household Heads in Northern Coahuila (Migration Selectivity)

Characteristic (Variable)	Non-migrant Household Heads	Migrant Household Heads		All House-hold Heads
		Dormant (before 1985)	Active (1985 & after)	
Number of HH heads in sample (n)[a]	321	86	53	460
% of sample HH heads	69.8	18.7	11.5	100.0
% Male	85.4	98.8	94.3	88.9
Age				
34 and younger	30.5	14.8	47.2	29.4
35–50	34.5	55.7	41.5	39.4
50 and older	35.1	29.5	11.3	31.3
Total	100.0	100.0	100.0	100.1
Education				
Less than 3 years	15.4	17.0	9.4	15.0
3–5 years	16.3	28.4	22.6	19.3
6 years and more	68.3	54.5	67.9	65.7
Total	100.0	99.9	99.9	100.0
Occupation in Mexico				
Agriculture	6.7	19.0	7.5	9.2
Unskilled urban	67.6	63.1	75.0	67.4
Skilled urban	7.7	9.5	7.5	8.0
Profess./tech.	17.9	8.3	10.0	15.4
Total	99.9	99.9	100.0	100.0
% Living in rural areas (< 5,000 pop.)	7.1	12.5	7.5	8.2
% Married[b]	84.5	93.2	98.1	87.7
Number of HH members				
Fewer than 4 (%)	38.6	34.1	34.0	37.2
4–7 (%)	50.0	48.9	58.5	50.8
8 and more (%)	11.4	17.0	7.5	12.0
Total	100.0	100.0	100.0	100.0
Stage of life cycle				
Single or married w/o children	1.9	4.5	0.0	2.2
All children < 13	37.2	23.9	50.0	36.1
Some children 13 and above	24.4	44.3	38.5	29.8
All children 13 and above	36.6	27.3	11.5	32.0
Total	100.1	100.0	100.0	100.1

a. Total households by migrant category. Different variables have different numbers of missing cases.
b. Including "free unions."

Coahuila (its maquiladoras hire mainly women; see Jones 1994) than in Zacatecas. Second, even in the absence of economic need, many young Coahuilan men travel to the United States as an "adventure." In our interviews we encountered many Coahuilans who had gone to the United States for a short time as youths but had never subsequently returned there.

This type of migrant did not often appear in Zacatecas, where economic necessity compelled the migration.

Compared to nonmigrants, active migrants in Coahuila are better educated, and most of them work in unskilled urban occupations. Again, the higher level of education among the active migrants is principally due to their younger ages; that is, they have been educated more recently, in a time of better facilities and higher standards. Their occupations in Mexico reflect the nature of the country's northern region, where most people live in urban areas. Fewer agricultural workers migrate from northern Coahuila than from Zacatecas. The underclass in the north is the unskilled urban proletariat, not the peasant class as in central and southern Mexico. Agriculture in northern Mexico is more like that in the United States—commercial, private, with large ranches and commercial grain or horticultural operations. In northern Coahuila, these operations tend to be family run and prosperous. Nor does the local professional and technical class generate much migration to the United States. Instead, the principal sources of U.S. migrants are the working classes in the mining and manufacturing industries of the region—those who are most vulnerable to downturns in steel production and its linked industries—and the urban service sectors that provide inputs for them or goods and services for their employees.

Active migrants tend to be married with preteen children, a fact that points to the same motivating forces as found in Zacatecas—the pressing need of young fathers to provide for their families' expanding needs. It also spawns the same results—U.S. migration at a time when the children may be in most need of a father's guidance. However, neither the impacts of migrant remittances nor those of paternal absence are as profound in Coahuila as in Zacatecas. This is because the Coahuilan family sends fewer members on fewer trips for less time. Migration thus has fewer impacts, positive or negative, there than in Zacatecas.

The Study Municipios Compared

Morelos and San Juan de Sabinas municipios represent the two faces of northern Coahuila's economy—commercial agriculture and small businesses; mining and heavy manufacturing. Taken together, their U.S. migration rate is markedly less than that of central Zacatecas (last column of table 3.6). Furthermore, internal migration is also substantially less. The lower levels of both U.S. and internal migration point again to the existence of alternative local employment opportunities for households in

Table 3.6 Migration Comparisons for Municipios in Northern Coahuila

	Morelos (commercial agric.)	S. Juan Sabinas (extrac./ urban)	Total (both mcpos.)
Migration Experience, All Households			
Number of households in sample (n)	227	239	466
% of HHs with U.S. migration experience[a]	55.1	29.7	42.1
% of HHs with active U.S. migrant[b]	29.1	18.4	26.3
% of HHs with 5 yrs.+ of U.S. migration[c]	18.9	13.0	15.9
% of HHs with 4+ work trips to U.S.[d]	22.9	12.1	17.4
% of migrant HHs with 1st trip < 1965	26.9	17.0	23.8
% of migrant HHs with all undocumented[e]	62.8	55.7	60.3
% of all HHs with active mexican migrant	4.0	6.3	5.2
Demographic Characteristics of Migrant vs. Nonmigrant Household Heads (Selectivity Analyses)			
Active migrant households:			
% of heads 34 years old and younger	40.5	62.5	47.2
% of heads with 3 yrs. education & more	86.5	100.0	90.6
% of heads who work in agriculture	12.0	0.0	7.5
% of heads who are rural	8.1	6.3	7.5
% of HHs with 8 members and more	10.8	0.0	7.5
% of HHs with all children < 13	44.4	62.5	50.0
Nonmigrant households:			
% of heads 34 years old and younger	37.3	26.1	30.5
% of heads with 3 yrs. education & more	79.4	87.9	84.6
% of heads who work in agriculture	15.8	1.0	6.7
% of heads who are rural	12.7	3.5	7.1
% of HHs with 8 members and more	12.8	10.6	11.4
% of HHs with all children < 13	43.0	33.7	37.2
Migrant percentage minus nonmigrant percentage:			
% of heads 34 years old and younger	3.2	36.4	16.7
% of heads with 3 yrs. education & more	7.1	12.1	6.0
% of heads who work in agriculture	− 3.8	− 1.0	0.8
% of heads who are rural	− 4.6	2.8	0.4
% of HHs with 8 members and more	− 2.0	− 10.6	− 3.9
% of HHs with all children < 13	− 1.4	28.8	12.8
SELECTIVITY INDEX(ES)[f]	.055	.233	.105

a. "Actuality"
b. "Recency
c. "Quantity"
d. "Frequency"
e. On latest trip; includes only migrants with at least one U.S. trip.
f. $\Sigma i; |M_i - N_i| / \Sigma_i |M_i + N_i|$, where M_i = the % figure for migrant households on selectivity characteristic i; and N_i = the % figure for nonmigrant households on selectivity characteristic i.

northern Coahuila. Nevertheless, over 40 percent of the households surveyed had some U.S. migration experience.

Given their economic differences, it is not surprising that the two study municipios in Coahuila have different migration levels and that migration selectivity also differs between them. Morelos has a considerably higher level of U.S. migration than San Juan de Sabinas (Nueva Rosita) (table 3.6, columns 1 and 2). Its high migration rate is apparently due to its kinship ties with Texas, to its agribusiness economy, and to its relatively small population. In its level of migration experience, Morelos is remarkably similar to Luis Moya, the commercial agricultural center in Zacatecas (table 3.3). In both places, the seasonal and year-to-year variations in agricultural production generate periodic push forces that propel migration to the United States. Their small populations result in a limited variety of employment opportunities and a leakage of income away from the city (see Jones 1991). In its dependence upon U.S. dollars, Morelos is something like a progressive commercial agricultural town in central Mexico that has been transplanted to northernmost Mexico.

Nueva Rosita is a very different sort of place, with not only a lower rate of U.S. migration than Morelos, but greater selectivity as well (table 3.6). Compared to nonmigrants, active migrants are exceptionally young and well educated, heading small households with very young children. Thus, the profile that emerges is that of a young, educated, and semiskilled urban proletariat whose jobs have been pulled from underneath them by deteriorating economic conditions. Facing these difficulties, they have crossed the border, usually illegally, to take urban, unskilled jobs in the United States.

Conclusions

Both central Zacatecas and northern Coahuila have high rates of U.S. migration. In both regions, U.S. migration rates have risen inexorably in recent decades, except for short dips owing to U.S. immigration restrictions and to large-scale Mexican agricultural and industrial programs. Agricultural work accounted for most U.S. jobs in the pre-1965 period; afterward, migrants worked predominantly in unskilled urban jobs: in restaurants and factories, in construction and housework. U.S. migrants today, from both regions, are predominantly illegal. Migrants from both regions differ from nonmigrants—a greater proportion are male; they are younger and better educated; and more are married with small children. This pattern of migration selectivity is explained in large part by the arduous nature of the migration experience and the pressing economic needs of growing families.

Central Zacatecas has a higher rate of U.S. migration than Coahuila, however, because of the poorer economic condition of the region as well as its longer tradition of U.S. migration. Migrants tend to go to California, although Texas is much closer, because of the better employment and legal climate in California. They come from agricultural jobs in rural areas of Mexico; in the United States, they end up in unskilled jobs in urban areas. Therefore, they undergo some upward occupational mobility, although once they reach the urban areas, this mobility is thwarted. Within central Zacatecas, both U.S. migration rates and selectivity are lower for the commercial agricultural municipio (Luis Moya) than for the subsistence agricultural municipio (Villanueva) or the diversified local business center (Jerez), where migration occurs in response to reinvestment goals rather than to economic distress.

Northern Coahuila's lower U.S. migration rate is due to the more dynamic and diversified nature of the region's economy. Migrants tend to travel to Texas owing to proximity and to their strong kinship ties to the state. In migrating, they tend to move from unskilled urban jobs in Mexico to unskilled urban jobs in the United States, thus experiencing little occupational mobility; however, after reaching urban areas they are able to progress into skilled jobs more readily than are migrants from Zacatecas. The two municipios within the region illustrate different migration levels and motivations. The commercial agricultural center of Morelos sends more migrants because of its traditionally strong U.S. ties and its lack of employment alternatives, but its homogeneous labor force structure means that selectivity is relatively low. The mining and manufacturing center of Nueva Rosita has lower migration levels owing to its size and diversity, but it exhibits high selectivity due to the existence of an educated urban proletariat class whose members are forced to migrate by episodic layoffs in the coal and metallurgical industries.

4

U.S. Migration and Household Economic Behavior

Now we come to the crux of the analysis and seek answers to many of the questions posed in chapter 1. Do migrant households live disconnected from their own communities—dependent upon remittances, consuming but not investing, spending their money outside the community, and alienated from local culture? Is theirs a disconnected lifestyle like that of long-distance commuters? Or are they in fact integrated into the local community, spending and investing there and taking part in community life, reinvigorated by the hope for a better life that foreign earnings bring them? Does migration create an unequal rural society, with a migrant bourgeoisie and a nonmigrant commoner class? Or does it create a more egalitarian (though dichotomized) rural society—with a nonmigrant group that depends upon local resources and a migrant group at the same economic level that lives on foreign remittances? Is migration as important to the economic welfare of families in northern Mexico as it is to those of central Mexico?

In this chapter, both the recency and the quantity of household migration are considered. In terms of recency, households in which at least one member worked in the United States in the three years prior to 1988 are considered active; others are termed inactive. In terms of quantity, five categories classify families along a continuum from nonmigrant (zero years working in the United States cumulated by all family members), to long-term migrant (more than ten years). These two indicators complement one another. Recency provides a clear tie to current economic status; quantity reflects the longer-term impact on income, possessions, and household behavior attributable to migration over a number of years.

Central Zacatecas
Migration and Economic Welfare

If we assume that migrants remit earnings, that these remittances translate into household income and possessions, and that this behavior involves a high proportion of the migrant households (and there is clear evidence for these assumptions in Zacatecas), then we would expect a positive relationship between migration and a household's economic status. This is just what the data show. The active migrant household was nearly twice as likely to earn 4 million pesos or more in 1987 ($2,850 U.S.) as was the inactive household (table 4.1). Analogously, the long-term migrant household was more than twice as likely to earn 4 million pesos as the nonmigrant household. Furthermore, as households accumulated more and more years of work in the United States, their income increased. The exception to this is that in the first two years of migration, there was actually a drop in income—that is, short-term migrant households (which had cumulated less than two years of U.S. work time) earned less than nonmigrants. This finding offers us valuable insight into how migration experience is translated into family income. During the first two years, migration yields less income for the family, as first-time migrants struggle to find their niches in the U.S. labor market. They often start in low-paying but readily available jobs in

Table 4.1 Household Income and Possessions and U.S. Migration: Central Zacatecas

	Recency of Migration		Quantity of Migration					
	Pre-1985: Inactive	1985 and after: Active	None (non-migrant)	Up to 2 years (Short-term)	2–5 years (Med. short-term)	5–10 years (Med. long-term)	>10 years (Long-term)	All HHs
No. of households	363	233	183	98	138	66	111	596
% of households that are high income[a]	24.7	46.3	25.6	22.7	31.1	41.5	52.8	33.2
Sewing machine	53.2	56.0	49.2	50.0	50.7	60.0	67.6	54.3
Stereo	32.0	35.3	31.7	34.7	27.0	30.3	44.5	33.3
Television	83.2	89.7	80.9	83.7	84.8	95.5	91.0	85.7
Washing machine	40.8	45.1	39.9	33.7	35.5	48.5	60.4	42.4
Refrigerator	42.1	56.0	49.2	50.0	50.7	60.0	67.6	54.3
Truck	20.9	32.2	16.9	23.5	25.4	31.8	36.9	25.3
5+ rooms in home	38.6	40.8	38.3	28.6	39.9	47.0	45.9	39.4
Non-dirt floor	92.8	95.7	92.8	92.9	93.4	93.8	97.3	93.9
7 hect. + of land	24.3	32.3	21.3	23.5	30.4	27.3	37.6	27.4

a. Family income of at least 4 million pesos in 1987.

rural areas (see also Jones and Murray 1986). Furthermore, the debts for initial transportation, documents, and settling in must be paid. As a result, family incomes remain low for the first two years. Then remittances start to flow back to the family in larger amounts, providing income and creating a savings pool for consumption and investment.

There is still another reason that newly migrating families earn less than nonmigrant families: many of the nonmigrant families are members of the local professional and social elite. Owing to their positions in the community, this group commands the highest local incomes, and they inflate the proportion of nonmigrant households earning over 4 million pesos. Nevertheless, at some time between two and five years of migration experience, the migrant household is able to surpass the median earnings of the nonmigrant group, including the local elite. After that, the migrant household rapidly outdistances the nonmigrant one.

U.S. migration enables households to purchase various major and minor appliances, trucks, land, and home improvements. As the U.S. work years accumulate, so do the possessions (table 4.1). The purchases for which the relationship is parabolic or flat over the first three categories—that is, ownership goes down and then up, or remains the same—include four major purchases that are "lumpy" (costly and indivisible) and thus require substantial savings prior to purchase: washing machine, refrigerator, room additions (five or more rooms in the house), and new floor ("non-dirt floor"). During the first two years, enough income is available for small purchases such as stereos or television sets; but not for these major purchases. After three years of cumulated U.S. earnings, the larger items may be purchased, although the proportion of spending they account for may not increase until five or even ten years of migration experience is cumulated. By way of example, in 1987 a television could be purchased new in Mexico for around $70; however, a new refrigerator cost at least $300. Truck purchases are an exception to the rule—they increase right away despite being lumpy. This is because a used truck can be purchased in the United States early in the migration process, used for a while there, and then driven home to Mexico. Nevertheless, long-term migrant households do have many more trucks than do short-term households.

These results leave little doubt that U.S. migration significantly betters the economic lot of families in central Zacatecas, and they support those of previous studies in nearby Jalisco and Michoacán (Massey et al. 1987; Reichert and Massey 1979; Shadow 1979). It should be noted that the results reported here identify higher levels of possessions than did the earlier studies; for example, 86 percent of central Zacatecas households in the present study had televisions, compared to 69 percent in Altamira, Jalisco (Massey et al. 1987, 228), and 60 percent in Chamitlán, Michoacán (Massey et al. 1987). This may be due to a combination of the somewhat higher population in the municipios studied here and the five years intervening between the two studies, during which time economic conditions have improved in Zacatecas.

U. S. Migration and "Consumption" Versus "Investment"

Granted that families with recent and long-standing migration experience are much better off economically than those without it, does this experience result in nothing more than conspicuous consumerism, while productive investment languishes?

The data show the reverse to be true. More recent migration experience correlates with more household investment (chiefly in agriculture) than does past migration experience; the more U.S. migration, the greater the investment (table 4.2). The proportion of expenditures that go toward mixed consumption and investment purchases, notably home improvements and medical care, also tends to increase with migration. The proportion accounted for by consumption declines. More than two-thirds of both inactive and nonmigrant household expenditures go toward consumption, compared to around one-half for active and long-term migrant households. Active and long-term migrant households invest at twice the rate of inactive and nonmigrant households.

An examination of individual expenditures suggests that the need for and cost of an item may help determine when in the migration process it is purchased (table 4.2). Owing to their poverty, nonmigrant households must spend more than half their budgets on food, but long-term migrant households spend scarcely one-third. Short-term and long-term migrants spend about the same portion of their budget on clothing, which is purchased in incremental quantities at all points in the migration process. Appliances and furniture, due to their relatively high unit costs, are saved for later on, and in fact long-term households spend the most on them. However, these items still constitute only 5 percent of expenses, compared to 35 percent for food and 10 percent for clothing.

Long-term migrant households spend twice as much on home purchases and improvements as do nonmigrant households (table 4.2). This is consistent with the need for time to save up enough money to add a room,

Table 4.2 Household Expenditures and U.S. Migration: Central Zacatecas

| Expenditure | Recency of Migration | | Quantity of Migration | | | | | |
	Pre-1985: Inactive	1985 and after: Active	None (non-migrant)	Up to 2 years (Short-term)	2-5 years (Med. short-term)	5-10 years (Med. long-term)	>10 years (Long-term)	All HHs
No. of households	363	233	183	98	138	66	111	596
Consumption	66.7	53.4	**69.9**	61.6	62.5	59.4	48.8	60.2
Food	51.4	38.9	**58.3**	46.3	46.1	41.9	34.7	45.3
Clothing	12.0	11.4	11.5	12.1	**13.3**	13.2	9.6	11.7
Appliances/furn.	3.3	3.1	.1	3.2	3.1	4.3	**4.5**	3.2
Mixed cons./inves.	21.6	28.1	17.9	22.8	26.5	24.3	**30.8**	24.8
Home purch./imprv.	10.8	15.1	8.1	10.4	14.5	**16.6**	15.7	12.9
Medical care	5.0	6.3	3.6	6.7	5.8	3.0	**8.0**	5.7
Education	3.8	3.3	**4.0**	3.4	3.0	3.5	3.6	3.5
Church	.4	.3	**.4**	**.4**	**.4**	**.4**	.3	.4
Community projects	.4	.3	.3	**.5**	.4	.2	.3	.3
Interest	1.2	2.8	1.5	1.4	2.4	.6	**2.9**	2.0
Investment	9.1	16.5	8.7	13.9	9.3	15.2	**17.8**	12.8
Agric. inputs	4.0	10.9	5.1	9.2	5.4	2.1	**12.5**	7.4
Truck purchase	5.1	5.6	3.6	4.7	3.9	**13.1**	5.3	5.4
Miscellaneous	2.6	2.1	**3.5**	1.7	1.7	1.1	2.6	2.3
Total	100.0	100.1	100.0	100.0	100.0	100.0	100.1	100.1

Stage (quantity) of migration in which highest percentage is recorded for a particular expenditure is indicated by **bold type.**

put in a floor, install a new roof, etc. Likewise, long-term migrant households spend proportionately more on medical care. These expenditures most often involve a visit to a doctor to handle a medical emergency for an aging parent or a sick child. Such a visit is almost entirely dependent on savings, because it is expensive, and Mexican doctors and hospitals generally require payment immediately. In addition, the long-term household pays out much more in interest than the nonmigrant household, which is consistent with larger purchases made on credit later in the migration process. Households do not differ much in their expenditures on educational supplies for children and their monetary support of the church or community.

Long-term migrant households spend markedly more on agricultural inputs and trucks than do nonmigrant or beginning migrant households. Agricultural machinery, land, and chemicals are expensive, requiring considerable savings which may take years to accumulate. The same holds for a truck. Although some trucks are purchased early on, most are purchased after five years of U.S. migration experience (table 4.2).

Because food purchases so dominate the household spending pattern, we recalculated household expenditures, excluding the amount spent on food. The resulting figures showed a very similar pattern to that found in table 4.2. Consumption declines while investment increases with increased U.S. migration. Mixed consumption/investment increases less strongly, but the "peaks" in percentages are basically in the same places. Therefore, the basic conclusion is not simply that with migration families are able to spend less on food and more on everything else. It is that U.S. migration enables them to meet planned, sequential consumption and investment goals.

The most important conclusion from the foregoing data, from the point of view of the debate between structuralists and functionalists, is that investments increase strikingly with migration. Looking at the disaggregated data on agricultural input expenditures, we find that they are not limited to a few exceptional households but are distributed over many households: 47 of the 161 active migrant households whose heads worked in agriculture spent money on agricultural inputs in 1987, and 15 of them spent one million pesos (U.S. $714) or more. Major purchases included machinery (chiefly tractors), land, insecticides, fertilizers, and seeds. The average active household spent 451,000 pesos ($322) on agricultural inputs in 1987, compared to 111,000 pesos ($79) for the average inactive household. These findings are important because they indicate that far from disinvesting in family rural livelihoods, active migrant households use U.S. dollars to sustain and improve them.

It is notable that the tendency of migrants to donate large amounts to community projects, seen in some studies, is not evident here. In general, U.S. dollars are not being channeled into community projects or local churches. Together, these account for less than 1 percent of family expenditures, regardless of the migration experience of the household (table 4.2). Evidently, the direct beneficiaries of U.S. migration in central Zacatecas are families, not community institutions.

As for investment in family-run businesses, there is partial evidence that the incidence of family business ownership is higher among households with more U.S. migration experience (table 4.3). It is not true that more

Table 4.3 Percentage of Households Owning a Family Business, by U.S. Migration Experience: Central Zacatecas

| | Recency of U.S. Migration | | Quantity of U.S. Migration | | | |
	Inactive %	Active %	< 2 years (Beginner and non-migrant) %	2 years & more (Advanced migrant) %	Overall %	n
All households	12.5	9.9	11.8	11.2	11.5	593
Urban households[a]	13.5	13.8	11.7	15.5	13.6	206
Rural households[b]	11.9	8.3	11.9	9.0	10.3	387

a. Includes households in the county seats of Villanueva and Jerez.
b. Includes households in all other localities.

recent (active) households own more such businesses than inactive households. In fact, the reverse is the case, in particular for rural areas. This is understandable because the lack of market thresholds for goods and of business infrastructure keeps businesses from succeeding in small Mexican towns. There is a very slight tendency for active families to have more urban businesses than the inactive families. But consider that recent migration may not encompass a large enough time frame for cumulating remittances to invest in a family business. When we examine urban families with two or more years of cumulated U.S. migration experience, we see that they own significantly more family businesses than those with less than two years (table 4.3, second panel). These investments do not stand out like the rural household's agricultural investments do, in part because they are usually a sideline rather than the family's chief source of income. Long-term U.S. migration enables urban families such as those in Jerez to save up and start a small market, a restaurant, a pharmacy, or a photographic studio, to be run by the rest of the family to supplement income from the household head's regular job and from migration.

To summarize, U.S. migration brings not only a higher level of possessions and property, but a higher relative level of expenditures on agricultural investments, family human capital investments such as home improvements and medical care, and urban family businesses. These items reinforce family productivity in the long run and should be considered as mechanisms of family economic survival. The data show little evidence of ostentatious or frivolous expenditures; nor in the open-ended part of the survey did respondents mention wasteful household purchases as a problem of their own or other families. A functionalist conclusion seems appropriate in this case: U.S. migration results in investment in rural livelihoods, not disinvestment. Focusing on the individual family, we conclude that both economic improvement and considerable investment are the rule, just as suggested in table 1.1 (a and d) and the discussion in chapter 1. Migration enables households to survive in the difficult physical and economic environment whose characteristics were laid out in chapter 2. Nevertheless, we cannot conclude that U.S. migration is beneficial from a social or community perspective. It does not result in increased levels of monetary support to community institutions such as the church or to community projects (which, under the Solidarity or PRONASOL program, rely on community contributions and labor). Social impacts on the family may be negative (absence of the father, disparagement of local institutions and values) or on the other hand they may be positive (renewed hope for the future, increased social status and autonomy). Our survey does not provide adequate data to support such judgments.

The "Externalization" of Household Expenditures

Do migrant remittances drain away from the local economy because migrants spend their earnings outside the town and local region? The data present mixed evidence on this question. Yes, advanced U.S. migrant households spend significantly more outside of their home town (locality) than do other households; but no, most of these expenditures do not leave the local region (municipio).

Active and advanced migrant households do spend significantly more outside of their locality than inactive, beginning, or nonmigrant households (table 4.4a). Whether we consider consumption, investment, or mixed expenditures—or any individual item within these categories— U.S. migration experience leads to more expenditures outside the locality. There are two principal reasons for this: first, among migrant families some goods are purchased in the United States; and second, migrant families are more likely to have a vehicle with which they can shop in a nearby town or city. (To be exact, the proportion of active migrant families with a truck is 32 percent, compared to only 17 percent for nonmigrant families.) From the "village" perspective, then, externalization of expenditures does occur, and this leakage of money will have a negative effect on the local growth multiplier for the town.

However, only a fraction of the money spent by migrant families outside their home locality is also spent outside the municipio. Most rural families,

Table 4.4a Percentage of Expenditures Made Outside Home Locality, by Recency and Quantity of U.S. Migration: Central Zacatecas

Selected Expenditures[a]	Recency of Migration		Quantity of Migration		Overall	n
	Inactive	Active	< 2 years (Beginner and non-migrant)	2 years & more (Advanced migrant)		
Consumption	20.3	42.5	19.5	36.7	29.1	v[b]
Food	13.9	35.3	14.4	29.3	22.3	512
Clothing	39.7	60.7	39.9	54.9	47.8	546
Appliances/furn.	49.3	66.0	51.1	59.5	56.5	124
Mixed cons./inves.	33.9	58.4	35.9	50.8	44.4	v
Home purch./imprv.	25.2	56.9	26.6	47.0	38.5	260
Medical care	61.1	70.7	63.9	66.0	65.1	358
Education	21.0	34.6	21.7	30.7	26.5	389
Interest	40.0	66.7	39.3	65.8	54.5	66
Investment	47.8	69.5	50.4	61.5	57.3	v
Agric. inputs	45.0	57.8	45.5	52.8	50.5	105
Truck purchase	50.0	92.3	58.3	71.4	66.7	33
Total, selected expends.	25.8	51.6	26.1	44.0	36.5	v

a. Minor and miscellaneous expenses are not considered.
b. v = Variable sample sizes depending on subcategory.

for example, spend their money in the *cabecera*, or "county seat" of their municipio (table 4.4b). Many "convenience" items—such as home building materials, used appliances and furniture, and agricultural inputs such as seeds, animals, and land—can be supplied adequately in the county seat. Advanced migrant households make only 16 percent of their total expenditures outside their municipio, compared to 44 percent outside of their locality (compare tables 4.4b and 4.4a). Sixteen percent is a low figure, particularly when viewed in light of previous research in the United States, where out-of-county expenditure figures of over 50 percent and out-of-town figures of over 80 percent are common for towns that, like the ones studied here, are in the shadow of a metropolitan area (see Jones 1991). In central Zacatecas, clearly most family expenditures remain within the local municipio, where they are recirculated to improve local economic growth.

Regardless of household migration experience, investment goods are

Table 4.4b Percentage of Expenditures Made Outside Home Municipio, by Recency and Quantity of U.S. Migration: Central Zacatecas

Selected Expenditures[a]	Recency of Migration		Quantity of Migration		Overall	n
	Inactive	Active	< 2 years (Beginner and non-migrant)	2 years & more (Advanced migrant)		
Consumption	7.7	9.8	6.1	10.4	8.6	v[b]
Food	3.3	6.0	2.9	5.7	4.4	512
Clothing	20.3	19.4	19.0	20.9	20.0	546
Appliances/furn.	29.6	22.6	24.4	27.8	26.6	124
Mixed cons./inves.	15.6	15.9	17.6	14.3	15.9	v
Home purch./imprv.	7.3	10.1	10.1	7.3	8.5	260
Medical care	39.8	33.4	40.5	34.5	37.2	358
Education	6.0	8.3	6.5	7.3	6.9	389
Interest	20.0	16.7	17.9	18.4	18.2	66
Investment	36.1	34.6	29.7	39.2	34.7	v
Agric. inputs	18.3	8.9	12.1	15.3	14.3	105
Truck purchase	50.0	84.7	58.3	66.7	62.7	33
Total, selected expends.	12.8	15.7	10.9	15.5	13.8	v

a. Minor and miscellaneous expenses are not considered.
b. v = Variable sample sizes depending on subcategory.

more likely to be externally purchased than mixed goods, and mixed goods more so than consumption goods. Investments (e.g., truck, and agricultural inputs), shopping goods (e.g., clothing and appliances), and highly specialized services (medical care) are externally purchased more often than convenience goods (food) and everyday services (education). This is of course a function of the availability of goods and services in larger versus smaller places and of the better quality of such items in the larger places.

These data lend some support to the structural arguments and some to the functional arguments with regard to externalization of household expenditures. At the local scale of analysis (table 1.1c), the village loses some proportion of its remittances from U.S. migration, because the migrant family is more mobile and able to shop in cities and towns elsewhere—just as structuralists suggest. However, the municipio recaptures most of these remittances and they are recirculated within the region—as the functionalists suggest. With respect to stage of migration (table 1.1e), there is little doubt that as U.S. migration progresses, more money is externalized. However, this trend is much more pronounced for the town than for the municipio.

U.S. Migration and Income Inequalities

The question of how migration affects income inequalities has generated considerable discussion in the literature and still has not been resolved, in part because of the lack of good indicators for inequality. Furthermore, whether inequality increases or decreases with U.S. migration depends on both the scale of analysis and on the stage of migration. At the advanced stage represented by central Zacatecas, we may expect that migrants are somewhat above average in income (relative to others in their hometowns) and thus that U.S. migration has the effect of increasing economic inequalities among families within the villages. But what of inequalities between urban and rural areas? We would expect these to be decreasing, because the more backward rural areas have higher rates of U.S. migration.

A major difficulty in testing these expectations in the present study is that we have no longitudinal data that indicate household incomes in the sending region before and after U.S. migration. We have only current (1987) household income, coupled with current and past migration data. How do we estimate what the premigration income distribution looked like? The answer can be found using surrogate procedures for approximating income at different stages of the migration process. There are two separate questions to be answered: (1) What was the distribution of family income before migration, and from where in this distribution have U.S. migrant households come since then? (2) What were the relative levels of rural and urban income, both before and after migration?

The surrogate used for premigration family income in the first question is a household possessions index, defined by summing the following eight household possessions (a value of 1 is assigned if the household has the item, and a value of 0 if it does not): television, refrigerator, truck, sewing machine, stereo, non-dirt floor, more than 6 hectares of land, more than 4 rooms in the house. Owing to the long-term purchase of household possessions, most would have been bought prior to the most recent year (here, 1987) for which family income and remittances were obtained. The question may be answered by observing the scores on this possessions index of migrant households that received remittances in 1987.

The surrogate used for premigration income in the second question is the income in 1987 of nonmigrant households; this approximates the income situation the region would exhibit if no U.S. migration had taken place. Postmigration income is simply the 1987 income of all families in the sample; this gives the income situation with migration taken into account. The second question may be answered by comparing the average income of urban and rural residents for each of these two groups.

The conclusions tend to fit the expectations: U.S. migration increases interfamilial inequalities as a whole in the region, but reduces inequalities between rural and urban areas. Interestingly, households that received remittances in 1987 fall at all levels on the possessions index (fig. 4.1). It is evident from these data that U.S. migration as an economic strategy is not limited to a narrow elite but is an option open to households at all points

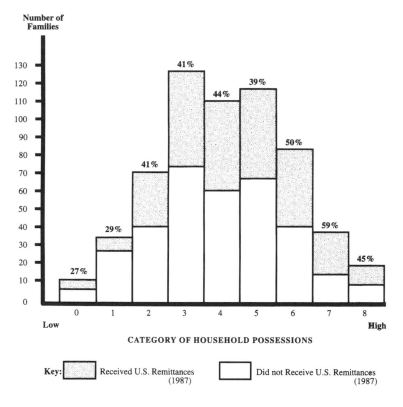

Figure 4.1 Distribution of families by category of total household possessions: Central Zacatecas

on the income spectrum. Closer inspection does show, however, that remittance-receiving families are somewhat more concentrated above the mean than below it. The implication is that recent remittances have increased the income differential among families of the region.

By contrast, the income differences between urban and rural areas of the region have declined as a function of U.S. migration (table 4.5, first column). Among nonmigrating households—whose situation is our surrogate for premigration conditions—the average rural family earned 2.6 million pesos in 1987, while the average urban family earned 3.7 million—40 percent more. Among all households, whose behavior is our surrogate for postmigration conditions, the average rural family earned 3.9 million pesos while the average urban family earned 4.0 million—only 2 percent more (see ratios of urban to rural incomes, table 4.5). In other words, as a result of U.S. migration, rural incomes have almost overtaken

Table 4.5 Family Income by Size of Place and U.S. Migration Status: Central Zacatecas

Migration Status of Family	Mean Family Income (1987, in thousands of pesos)	Std. Dev.	CV[a]	n
All places				
Overall[b]	3,945	4,805	1.218	585
Active families[c]	5,294	6,350	1.199	229
Inactive families[d]	3,078	3,187	1.035	356
Nonmigrant families	3,015	3,428	1.137	183
Urban places[e]				
Overall	4,005	3,676	.918	204
Active families[c]	4,547	3,570	.785	65
Inactive families	3,751	3,710	.989	139
Nonmigrant families	3,652	3,853	1.055	71
Rural places[f]				
Overall	3,913	5,316	1.359	381
Active families[c]	5,570	7,147	1.279	164
Inactive families	2,647	2,725	1.029	217
Nonmigrant families	2,611	3,079	1.179	112
Ratio of urban to rural income				
Overall	1.024			
Active families[c]	.813			
Inactive families	1.417			
Nonmigrant families	1.399			

a. The coefficient of variation, defined as the standard deviation divided by the mean.
b. Overall families include active families plus inactive families.
c. At least one family member has worked in the United States since 1984.
d. Inactive families include nonmigrant plus dormant families.
e. 5,000 people and above in 1980.
f. Fewer than 5,000 people in 1980.

urban incomes. (Table 4.5 also verifies the increasing differential in individual family incomes with U.S. migration; compare the coefficient of
variation—a measure of inequality—for nonmigrant families vs. overall.)

This exacerbation of inequalities between better-off and poorer families
supports the structuralists' scenario for towns at advanced stages of migration, such as those of central Zacatecas (table 1.1f). At the same time, the
income convergence between rural and urban areas supports the functionalists' scenario at the regional as opposed to the town scale of analysis
(table 1.1b).

These results lend conclusive support to neither the structural nor the
functional arguments. On the one hand individual families do move farther
apart on the income distribution. Supported by remittances, many poor
families vault over the mean, leaving the poor nonmigrant class far behind.
But this migration-induced mobility does not clump them together at the
high end of the income scale, as a homogeneous elite. Instead, they are
spread all over the upper half, and much of the lower half as well, of the
income distribution. Even the poor nonmigrant class, by virtue of overall
increases in local income due to migration, benefits in an absolute sense
even as it falls farther behind. It is difficult to draw negative conclusions
about a development that benefits so many families, most of them formerly
among the ranks of the poor.

Migration Versus Education As a Determinant of Income

Although our data do not allow us to gauge directly the social impacts of
migration, we can try to do so indirectly. Several authors point out that
U.S. migration leads to a disparagement of local values and institutions.
One of the most important local institutions is the educational system.
Does U.S. migration, by enabling a young person to bypass the educational
pathway to economic success, make education superfluous and devalue it
in the community? Just how much of a role does education play in the
income that a head of household in central Zacatecas is able to earn? How
much of a role does U.S. migration play? We have noted that U.S. migrants
have above-average educational levels for their region. Does education
continue to play an independent role in income attainment for these
migrants?

Simple bivariate relationships suggest that both migration and education contribute to a household head's higher income (figs. 4.2a and 4.2b).
The educated head of household (three years or more of schooling) is more

likely to earn 2 million pesos ($1,429 U.S.) or more per year than the un-educated one, and the active migrant household head (one who worked in the U.S. after 1984) is considerably more likely to earn this much than the inactive one. Among heads of household, about half of those who were uneducated and half of the inactive migrants earned 2 million pesos per year. However, 75 percent of active migrants but only 60 percent of the educated earned this amount, suggesting that migration is a surer path to economic success than education. Of course (and here is the problem) some of the income-enhancing effect of migration is due to higher educa-tion, which helps to motivate migration in the first place (see chapter 3). How do we separate out the effects of education and migration on income?

One way out of this entanglement is through the statistical procedures of the elaboration model (Johnson 1988, 191–221). This model offers a methodology by which the separate roles of independent variables may be

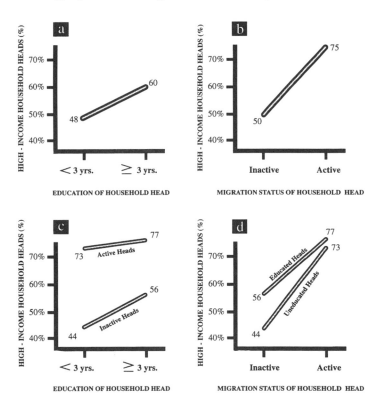

Figure 4.2 U.S. migration status and education as determinants of income: Central Zacatecas

discerned in multivariate relationships at the nominal level of analysis. Suppose that we focus for a moment only on the inactive migrant heads of household (in other words, we control for U.S. migration status). Since they have not migrated recently, we can assume that U.S. migration is not a factor in their current income level. Among this group, how much better off are those who are educated than those who are not? The answer is shown in figure 4.2c: 56 percent of those who are educated earn 2 million pesos and above, compared to only 44 percent of those who are uneducated—a difference of 12 percentage points. Clearly, then, education plays a role in income, independent of U.S. migration.

Now, suppose that we focus only on the uneducated heads of household (i.e., we control for education). For the uneducated, higher levels of income cannot be due to education. Among this group, how much better off are those with recent U.S. migration experience than those without it? The answer is shown in figure 4.2d: 73 percent of those who are active U.S. migrants earn 2 million pesos and above, compared to only 44 percent of those who are inactive—a difference of 29 percentage points. Therefore, we can say that U.S. migration plays a role in income, independent of education. We can also say that U.S. migration plays the greater role. Under these "controlled" conditions, its impact is 2.4 times as great ($29/12 = 2.42$).

When we focus on the better-off half of the controls (i.e., active and educated heads of household), the results are also revealing. Among the active migrant heads of household, education makes little difference in their incomes: 77 percent of the educated earn 2 million pesos, as compared to 73 percent of the uneducated (fig. 4.2c). Among the educated heads of household, however, U.S. migration plays a major role: 77 percent of the those who are active migrants earn 2 million pesos, as opposed to only 56 percent of those who are inactive (fig. 4.2d). Here, the relative impact of U.S. migration is greater than that of education by a factor of 5.3 ($21/4 = 5.25$).

Better education, therefore, makes a moderate difference in income when U.S. migration is unavailable or unpracticed by the household head. It may enable the person to gain a technical or professional position in the municipio capital or a nearby city. Better education is of scant help, however, to the U.S. migrant. We have seen that such migrants work predominantly in unskilled urban or rural jobs. Education matters little in the conduct of such work. Upon return to Mexico, education may help, in certain cases, in the wise reinvestment of migrant earnings in a family-run business or agricultural scheme. But its effect on income turns out to be relatively slight.

U.S. migration, then, is the great leveler; it brings relative success to the trained and the untrained alike. These results provide indirect quantitative evidence for an oft-stated claim: that U.S. migration negates the value of education and that U.S. migration may serve as a disincentive for the pursuit of education in Mexican towns with a high incidence of U.S. migration.

Northern Coahuila

Coahuila's demographic and economic profile (chapters 2 and 3) suggests that U.S. migration, although it is frequent, should be less crucial for family economic survival than in Zacatecas. Coahuilan families can choose from a portfolio of employment options—with the qualification that the urban, blue-collar nature of the Coahuila labor force means that households make relatively few agricultural investments and own few family businesses. Most people live in urban areas that offer substantial shopping opportunities, and U.S. shopping is often just a short drive away. Higher incomes enable more Coahuilans to have automobiles. Given the milieu in which they live, northern Coahuilans might be expected to depend on local work rather than remittances, to spend more heavily on consumer goods, to shop out of town, and in general to be more economically and socially mobile than central Zacatecans, with or without U.S. migration. In this section, we will see whether these expectations are supported by the evidence.

Migration and Economic Welfare

As expected, the data show that Coahuilan households depend far less on U.S. migration than is the case in Zacatecas. Some 60 percent of active and long-term migrant households in Coahuila earned 4 million pesos or more, compared to 50 percent of the inactive and nonmigrant households (table 4.6)—not even close to the two-to-one difference found in Zacatecas. This suggests that U.S. migration does play a role, but that it is a modest one. And as in Zacatecas, household income actually drops slightly for families with between zero and two years of cumulated work time in the United States, reflecting the period during which debts must be repaid and settling-in costs keep remittances low.

Household possessions show only a slight tendency to increase with U.S. migration experience. We might even say that inactive and short-term

Table 4.6 Household Income and Possessions vs. U.S. Migration: Northern Coahuila

	Recency of Migration		Quantity of Migration					
	Pre-1985: Inac-tive	1985 and after: Active	None (non-mi-grant)	Up to 2 years (Short-term)	2–5 years (Med. short-term)	5–10 years (Med. long-term)	> 10 years (Long-term)	All HHs
No. of households	356	110	265	86	44	26	45	466
% of households that are high income[a]	50.4	59.3	50.0	48.8	60.5	61.5	61.4	52.5
% of households having								
Sewing machine	45.9	45.5	45.8	47.7	45.5	57.7	35.6	45.8
Stereo	64.5	69.1	65.2	68.6	63.6	80.8	53.3	65.4
Television	92.1	91.8	92.4	87.2	93.2	96.2	95.6	92.0
Washing machine	66.5	68.2	67.4	60.5	68.2	76.9	68.9	66.9
Refrigerator	85.6	83.6	86.0	81.4	79.5	92.3	88.9	85.2
Truck	25.6	33.6	23.9	32.6	27.3	38.5	33.3	27.5
5+ rooms in home	44.7	51.8	49.4	31.4	45.5	57.7	51.1	46.4
Non-dirt floor	96.3	98.2	95.8	96.5	97.7	100.0	100.0	96.8
7 hect.+ of land	2.8	1.0	1.6	2.7	7.5	0	2.4	2.4

a. Family income of at least 4 million pesos in 1987.

migrant households have about the same level of possessions as active and long-term migrant households (table 4.6). Active households have somewhat more stereos, washing machines, and trucks, but the same level of sewing machines and televisions, and fewer refrigerators. The percentages for ownership of these possessions behave erratically with respect to migration experience. Furthermore, if there is any delay in purchase of the more expensive items (as in Zacatecas), the tendency is not very discernible here.

Evidently, as suggested earlier, Coahuilan migrants are not remitting as much as Zacatecas migrants, and Coahuilan households have several viable alternative employment opportunities, whereas those in Zacatecas do not. The scenario for this non-hearth region is as proposed in table 1.1g: U.S. migration has a relatively small impact on the family's economic situation.

U.S. Migration and "Consumption" Versus "Investment"

The data show clearly that Coahuilan households consume more and invest less than Zacatecan households. Consumption accounts for an average of 67 percent of the household budget (compared to 60 percent in Zacatecas), but this excludes the large "miscellaneous" category, most of which

Table 4.7 Household Expenditures and U.S. Migration: Northern Coahuila

| | Recency of Migration | | Quantity of Migration | | | | | |
	Pre-1985: Inac-tive	1985 and after: Active	None (non-mi-grant)	Up to 2 years (Short-term)	2–5 years (Med. short-term)	5–10 years (Med. long-term)	> 10 years (Long-term)	All HHs
No. of households	356	110	265	86	44	26	45	466
Consumption	66.6	66.6	65.6	67.4	60.3	69.3	**75.4**	66.6
Food	51.3	52.5	49.8	55.5	48.5	48.6	**60.9**	51.6
Clothing	12.1	10.0	**12.6**	10.1	8.8	9.2	11.8	11.6
Appliances/furn.	3.2	4.1	3.2	1.8	3.0	**11.5**	2.7	3.4
Mixed cons./inves.	17.2	16.4	17.4	**20.0**	15.7	15.5	12.0	17.1
Home purch./imprv.	8.7	7.9	9.2	**9.6**	8.5	8.8	2.8	8.5
Medical care	3.0	3.6	3.0	3.3	1.1	2.5	**6.4**	3.2
Education	4.4	3.6	4.2	**6.2**	4.4	3.6	1.3	4.2
Church	.6	.9	.5	**5.5**	1.2	.4	1.2	.7
Community projs.	.3	.2	**.3**	.2	**.3**	.2	.1	.3
Interest	.2	.2	.2	**.3**	.2	0	.2	.2
Investment	5.2	3.9	6.2	1.9	**9.0**	.1	.9	4.9
Agric. inputs	4.9	3.3	5.8	1.5	**8.2**	.1	.9	4.5
Truck purchase	.3	.6	.4	.4	**.8**	0	0	.4
Miscellaneous	11.0	13.2	10.9	10.6	14.9	**15.1**	11.8	11.5
Total	100.0	100.1	100.1	99.9	99.9	100.0	100.1	100.1

Stage (quantity) of migration in which highest percentage is recorded for a particular expenditure category is indicated by **bold type.**

is accounted for by automobile purchases, bringing the consumption total well over 75 percent in Coahuila (table 4.7). The Coahuilan family spends 52 percent on food, compared to 45 percent for the Zacatecas family (compare to table 4.2), which is understandable given that the average Zacatecas family is rural and produces a portion of its own food supply. In Coahuila, the salaried labor force spends relatively less on medical care (a social "investment" that is covered by employer-provided insurance) and less on home improvements. Agricultural investments are of minor importance here, where more than 90 percent of the people live in urban areas; but even so, they are markedly lower for long-term migrant households.

As in Zacatecas, in Coahuila little is spent on the church or on community

Table 4.8 Percentage of Households Owning a Family Business, by U.S. Migration Experience: Northern Coahuila

| | Recency of U.S. Migration | | Quantity of U.S. Migration | | | |
| | | | < 2 years (Beginner and non-migrant) | 2 years & more (Advanced migrant) | | |
	Inactive %	Active %	%	%	Overall %	n
All households	19.4	17.3	19.4	17.4	18.9	465
Urban households[a]	19.1	17.5	19.2	17.3	18.7	427
Rural households[b]	22.6	14.3	21.2	20.0	21.1	38

a. Includes households in the county seats of Nueva Rosita and Morelos.
b. Includes households in all other localities.

projects. Donations to the church are more substantial in Coahuila, however, possibly due to the emergence of evangelical Protestantism with its more demanding approach to parishioner contributions.

The active or advanced migrant household—whether urban or rural—is less likely to own a family business than the inactive or beginner migrant household (table 4.8). This contrasts with the situation in Zacatecas, where in urban areas there was a tendency for advanced migrant families to invest more in such businesses (table 4.3). This is due to the more blue-collar, more mobile, less family-oriented nature of northern Coahuilan society.

In summary, through U.S. migration the Coahuilan household is pursuing a strategy of consumption rather than a strategy of economic survival. The Coahuilan household has more access to alternative employment; U.S. migration is not needed for economic survival or investment, but simply enables the family to purchase more expensive consumer goods. The Zacatecas household lacks access to such alternative jobs; U.S. migration is often necessary to enable it to continue as a viable economic unit. The expenditure patterns of the Coahuilan household are, it may be hypothesized, positioned somewhere between those of central Mexico and those of the United States.

The Externalization of Household Expenditures

Compared to Zacatecans, Coahuilan families make relatively few purchases outside their locality (table 4.9a). Overall, only 15 percent of expenditures in northern Coahuila were made outside the locality of residence, compared to 37 percent in central Zacatecas (compare to table 4.4a). This is

Table 4.9a Percentage of Expenditures Made Outside Home Locality, by Recency and Quantity of U.S. Migration: Northern Coahuila

Selected Expenditures[a]	Recency of Migration		Quantity of Migration			
			< 2 years (Beginner and non-migrant)	2 years and more (Advanced migrant)	Overall	
	Inactive %	Active %	%	%	%	n
Consumption	11.1	14.0	11.5	12.3	11.8	v[b]
Food	6.8	10.0	7.5	7.8	7.6	464
Clothing	24.7	30.1	24.5	30.9	26.1	439
Appliances/furn.	28.1	25.6	29.2	23.3	27.7	174
Mixed cons./inves.	21.7	19.2	18.1	19.7	21.2	v
Home purch./imprv.	19.1	16.9	18.0	20.9	18.7	279
Medical care	31.1	25.9	11.5	25.0	29.8	218
Education	20.8	18.6	23.0	12.2	20.4	315
Interest	14.3	0.0	13.6	0.0	10.3	29
Investment	42.3	47.0	45.9	48.8	46.4	v
Agric. inputs	41.2	55.6	44.1	44.4	44.2	43
Truck purchase	60.0	0.0	66.7	100.0	71.4	7
Total, selected expends.	14.9	16.4	14.8	15.1	15.0	v

a. Minor and miscellaneous expenses are not considered.
b. v = Variable sample sizes depending on subcategory.

logical given that in northern Coahuila, the population is concentrated in urban centers. The fact that these urban centers are usually the municipio capitals helps to explain why only 11 percent of household purchases are made outside of the municipio (table 4.9b). Most Coahuilans, therefore, live in towns and cities large enough to have considerable offerings of goods and services.

There is a visible tendency for the percentage of purchases made outside of the locality to increase as a family's migration experience increases (table 4.9a). For example, external clothing purchases rise from 25 percent for beginner households to 31 percent for advanced migrant households. Likewise, medical expenses incurred externally rise from 12 percent to 25 percent under the same conditions. These figures suggest that where the quality of goods and services is an important component of the shopping decision, mobile Coahuilan households are willing to travel some

Table 4.9b Percentage of Expenditures Made Outside Home Municipio, by Recency and Quantity of U.S. Migration: Northern Coahuila

| | | Recency of Migration | | Quantity of Migration | | | |
| | | | | < 2 years (Beginner and non- migrant) % | 2 years and more (Advanced migrant) % | | |
Selected Expenditures[a]		Inactive %	Active %			Overall %	n
Consumption		6.8	10.0	6.9	9.5	7.7	v[b]
Food		3.1	6.3	3.5	5.2	3.9	464
Clothing		18.1	25.2	17.1	28.2	19.9	439
Appliances/furn.		23.7	20.5	24.6	18.6	23.2	174
Mixed cons./inves.		17.0	16.1	16.7	16.9	16.8	v
Home purch./imprv.		14.6	17.0	13.7	19.4	15.1	279
Medical care		24.4	16.7	23.4	19.7	22.5	218
Education		16.7	14.3	18.4	9.5	16.3	315
Interest		14.3	0.0	9.1	0.0	6.9	29
Investment		28.4	26.5	32.3	10.2	28.2	v
Agric. inputs		26.5	22.2	29.4	11.1	25.6	43
Truck purchase		60.0	50.0	66.7	0.0	57.2	7
Total, selected expends.		10.0	11.8	10.3	10.7	10.5	v

a. Minor and miscellaneous expenses are not considered.
b. v = Variable sample sizes depending on subcategory.

distance for these items. Again, the active and advanced migrant households are expressing a strategy of consumption—that is, focusing on how to spend their salaried earnings to maximize quality of life.

U.S. Migration and Income Inequalities

As in Zacatecas, in Coahuila interfamilial inequalities are increased by migration (as indicated by the fact that the coefficient of variation of family income is higher for all families than for nonmigrant families; see table 4.10), but this increase is less pronounced than in Zacatecas. The interpretation of these figures is clouded, however, by the extreme mean incomes for some members of the (nonmigrating) "elite"; notice (table 4.10) that inactive and nonmigrant families average between 800,000 and 1 million pesos more annual income than active families—figures that clearly are in conflict with the income percentage figures in table 4.6 for these same categories of families.

Table 4.10 Family Income by Size of Place and U.S. Migration Status: Northern Coahuila

Migration Status of Family	Mean Family Income (1987, in thousands of pesos)	Std. Dev.	CV[a]	n
All places				
Overall[b]	4,550	4,232	.930	455
Active families[c]	3,984	4,582	1.150	108
Inactive families[d]	4,726	4,108	.869	356
Nonmigrant families	4,905	4,392	.895	263
Urban places[e]				
Overall	4,685	4,363	.931	417
Active families[c]	4,066	4,716	1.160	101
Inactive families	4,883	4,233	.867	316
Nonmigrant families	5,060	4,500	.889	242
Rural places[f]				
Overall	3,067	1,805	.589	38
Active families[c]	2,798	1,397	.499	7
Inactive families	3,128	1,900	.607	31
Nonmigrant families	3,126	2,255	.721	21
Ratio of urban to rural income				
Overall	1.528			
Active families[c]	1.453			
Inactive families	1.561			
Nonmigrant families	1.619			

a. The coefficient of variation, defined as the standard deviation divided by the mean.
b. Overall families include active families plus inactive families.
c. At least one family member has worked in the United States since 1984.
d. Inactive families include nonmigrant plus dormant families.
e. 5,000 people and above in 1980.
f. Fewer than 5,000 people in 1980.

The urban-rural income differential, as in Zacatecas, is lessened by U.S. migration, but only slightly. In the absence of such migration, urban households outearn rural households by 5.1 to 3.1 million pesos—a ratio of 1.62 (table 4.10, at bottom). With U.S. migration (considering all households), urban households are superior by 4.7 to 3.1 million—a ratio of 1.53. Unfortunately, the small number of rural households surveyed and the extreme overall skewness of the data make further interpretations hazardous.

Migration Versus Education As a Determinant of Income

In Coahuila, as in Zacatecas, both education and U.S. migration play a role in earnings. As judged from their slopes, the simple bivariate relationships are both weaker than in Zacatecas (figs. 4.3a and 4.3b). Moreover, and surprisingly, in Coahuila the educated household head has hardly any income advantage over the uneducated one; 81 percent of the educated earn 2 million pesos, compared to 79 percent of the uneducated (fig. 4.3a). However, the active migrant has a definite advantage over the inactive one: 88 percent of the former and 78 percent of the latter earn 2 million pesos annually (fig. 4.3b). Ignoring for the moment the role of education in migration, it would appear that U.S. migration is the surer of the two paths to economic mobility in Coahuila.

The results of the elaboration model for Coahuila offer further insights. First, consider the result when we control for U.S. migration status, which is the same as asking what the impact of education on earnings is for heads of household who have not (recently) migrated. The answer is, very little; 80 percent of educated household heads earn 2 million pesos, versus 78 percent of those who are uneducated (fig. 4.3c)—a minuscule, 2-point

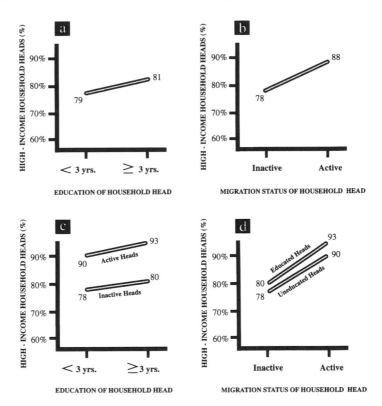

Figure 4.3 U.S. migration status and education as determinants of income: Northern Coahuila

differential. Education thus plays a lesser role in Coahuila than in Zacatecas; in Zacatecas, a better education enabled an inactive migrant to earn substantially more money than inactive household heads without this education, by a 12-percentage-point differential (fig. 4.2c). Next, consider the data when we control for education to determine the impact of recent migration on earnings for heads of household who are uneducated. In this case we find a moderate impact: 90 percent of the uneducated heads of household with active U.S. migration experience earn 2 million pesos, compared to 78 percent of those without migration experience (fig. 4.3d) —a 12-point differential. The relative importance of migration in comparison to education is indicated by the ratio of the two percentage differentials: U.S. migration is six times as important.

The better-off half of the controls (i.e., the active and the educated household heads) illustrates a similar conclusion. Among the active migrant heads, education increases the incidence of high income by only 3 percentage points. Among the educated heads, (recent) U.S. migration increases the incidence of high income by 13 percentage points. The relative importance of migration is indicated by the ratio 13:3; migration is 4.3 times as significant as education.

It is interesting that in a more progressive part of Mexico (northern Coahuila), the impact of education upon one's earning power is actually less than in a rather destitute region (central Zacatecas). However, although progressive, this area of Coahuila has relatively few professional, technical, or skilled urban positions (table 3.5); the work force is primarily blue-collar (mining and manufacturing). Employment in these "operative" positions is not dependent on education, but on family contacts and on one's willingness to take the job whatever the circumstances. A further explanation may be that the low threshold criterion used to divide the educated from the uneducated (three years or more of education) does not, in this relatively advanced region, very effectively identify those household heads with skills that command higher incomes.

Conclusions

Some authors have argued that a migrant elite is forming in rural central Mexico (Reichert 1981; Reichert and Massey 1979). The current findings—higher income and more possessions among a large group of active U.S. migrant households in nonmetropolitan central Zacatecas—suggests that not an elite but a broad-based middle class is forming in the region.

U.S. migration is increasing the distance between this new middle class and a residual cluster of poor nonmigrants; but it is also narrowing the economic gap between people in the rural areas and their urban neighbors. This new migrant class derives its strength from wage-labor earnings rather than from land, commerce, social class, and political patronage, which supported (and still support) the traditional elite. The replacement of a narrow social elite by a broad-based economic group, breaking the subservience of the peasant classes in rural Mexico, is a trend that would seem to bode well for the region. In other words, migration is an alternative economic mobility ladder in central Zacatecas.

Although economic development is slow in taking hold in these central rural areas, migration is enabling families to survive in place, to improve their standard of living, and to throw off the yoke of centuries of social and economic subjugation. If we are willing to extend the radius of impact to the municipio and beyond (to the whole state of Zacatecas, for example), there is little doubt that U.S. migration plays a significant role; that expenditures remain predominantly within the region (providing a substantial multiplier for local income growth); and that the region as a whole is improving its position in the national space economy.

For northern Coahuila, migration is less important for the attainment of income and possessions, for enabling investment, and for changing the distribution of income than it is in central Zacatecas. Both areas have a history of U.S. migration dating from the mid-1800s, and today the rate of active U.S. migration in both regions is high: 26 percent of the households of northern Coahuila and 39 percent of those in central Zacatecas have an active migrant. However, whereas U.S. remittances enable the average Coahuilan household to increase its income by some one-half million pesos, in Zacatecas the figure is over one million. Coahuilan households make few if any investments with their migrant earnings, but they do purchase significantly more consumer durable goods. Conversely, Zacatecas households make substantial investments and purchase more "human capital" goods than consumer durables. In Coahuila, as in Zacatecas, U.S. migration tends to reduce income inequalities between rural and urban areas.

In northern Coahuila, as elsewhere in the border region, economic activities—maquilas, commercial export agriculture, mining—are closely tied to those of the United States. This is the profile of an urbanized, formal-sector society. The U.S. lifestyle has also pervaded the region. U.S.-style shopping malls offer a wide range of U.S. goods. Late-model U.S. cars are seen everywhere. U.S. cable television is found in motels and restaurants. Transborder travel for work, shopping, and visiting relatives is common. Thus, U.S. migration is only one employment option among many; and consumption is more important than investment for the households of this region. For the great majority of families here, improving one's lifestyle is paramount. Increases in income are accompanied by more consumer expenditures, mostly within one's own urban area but also in the United States. It is ironic that in this more upwardly mobile society, education is still not very important in getting ahead. Individual economic progress is still strongly influenced by the family and political contacts that enable one to get a steady job.

The stronger channeling of remittances into central Zacatecas compared to northeastern Coahuila is narrowing the income gap between these two regions. For example, if we remove remittances from the income data for Zacatecas and Coahuila, we find that the average Coahuilan household earned (in 1987) almost 2 million pesos more than in Zacatecas; however, with migrant remittances, the Zacatecan household had moved to within about one million pesos of that in Coahuila.

Zacatecas and Coahuila are not unrepresentative of the larger picture of central versus border Mexico. Since the revolution, successive Mexican governments have tried to develop the interior; but the periphery (including the north as well as the far eastern and western coastal areas) has widened its economic dominance anyway—first with its cotton and cattle, later with commercial wheat and vegetables, later with oil and tourism, now with maquiladoras and border trade. U.S. wage labor may be the only major export sector that has managed to redistribute income effectively between regions and between urban and rural families in the country.

5

Case Studies of Household Heads

The following eight case studies—four in central Zacatecas and four in northern Coahuila—are representative of four different types of migrants found in both regions. For these narratives, the migration terminology from chapter 4 is employed, altered slightly to refer to the household head rather than to the whole household. The four types form a continuum from the contemporary, experienced migrant to the nonmigrant. *Long-term active* refers to a person with at least five years of cumulated U.S. migration experience, at least some of which was after 1984. *Short-term active* refers to a person with fewer than five years of such experience, some of which was post-1984. *Dormant* refers to a person who worked in the United States in 1984 or before. *Nonmigrant* refers to a person who never worked in the United States. These accounts are from eight follow-up interviews carried out a few days after the questionnaire survey. Either the household head or his wife was interviewed—both, in the case where both were present.

For each household, information was collected chronicling the life of the household head. The respondent was asked about early family life, education, and work; and about attitudes toward U.S. migration and its impacts on the local economy and on the family. Questions were asked concerning the initial and subsequent work trips to the United States, including reasons for going, the trip itself, the U.S. jobs and the money earned from them, the use of remittances, and other experiences.

The eight narratives that appear here were chosen because they best represent various positions on the continuum. The narratives go beyond this to illustrate how household characteristics are associated with U.S. migration, thus illustrating many of the findings of chapter 4. Names have been changed to hide the identity of the families. However, these are real families who lived in the locations indicated in the narratives. (For the sake of readability, all of the narratives use the present tense to discuss the families' characteristics at the time of the interviews, even though the interviews were conducted in 1988.)

Central Zacatecas
A Long-Term Active Migrant

Jesús Avila, 31 years old, lives with his wife Beatriz, 29, and their three children (ages 11, 9, and 7), in Ermita de Guadalupe, a town of around 3,000 people some 10 kilometers from Jerez, in Jerez municipio. Jesús is a farmer (*agricultor*) with 4 hectares of land, 2 of them irrigated. It is the family's fortune to have flat, fertile land in an irrigated zone, which frees them somewhat from the climatic problems of adjacent dryland farming areas. The land supports cattle as well as ample crops of corn and peaches, all of which the Avila family raises.

As of his latest U.S. job, in 1987, Jesús had gone to the United States eight times for a total working time of eight years there.

Jesús comes from an agricultural family, but his parents pushed him to finish *secundaria* (nine years of schooling). Nevertheless, at only 16 years of age, he followed the example of other boys from his town, marrying, quitting school, and moving in with his parents. Shortly afterward, in 1973, in order to support his wife and parents, he made his first trip to the United States, crossing the Río Grande as a mojado. He went initially to Chicago, where he worked as a room service delivery boy in a hotel. In all, he worked for some two years on this job, but the work was not continuous. He would work in the United States between September and April, returning to Mexico during the May through August period to help his family in the planting, cultivating, and harvesting of the crops. The money he earned enabled his family to buy cattle, thus diversifying their operation from subsistence corn and beans, to raising livestock for sale.

In 1977, Jesús and Beatriz began their family, with a daughter. A son followed in 1979, and another daughter in 1981. During this time, Jesús continued to migrate as a mojado, but he changed his destination to California, where he took various construction and agricultural jobs in smaller towns. U.S. migration had become a way of life for him—living in the United States one year and returning to Mexico the next. His earnings basically sustained his growing family.

In 1985, Jesús reached another watershed in his life. Following the example of many other farmers in the municipio, he used his savings from his U.S. work to purchase of some 100 peach seedlings, which he planted on

2 hectares of his land. As he put it, "I began to realize that others did this [planted peaches] and earned good income. I told myself that if others could do so, so could I." In 1987, the peach trees yielded their first small crop of peaches. With the peach earnings, plus savings from his work in the United States, in 1987 Jesús was able to purchase a used truck for 4 million pesos ($2,900 U.S. at the mid-1987 exchange rate). This truck enabled his father and him to purchase seeds and fertilizers at bulk outlets in Zacatecas, transporting them back home at considerable savings from what they had been paying in Ermita de Guadalupe and Jerez.

Jesús continues to migrate to the United States to sustain his peach and cattle operations, but their success will make it possible (and necessary) for him to curtail his U.S. work. This success is just beginning, with the first peach harvest and the purchase of the truck. The family in 1987 had some 12 million pesos of earnings (about $8,600, including almost $8,000 in U.S. remittances).

Jesús stated that "I sustain myself with money which I save from the U.S. . . . If I [were to] stay more than three years in my house, I [would be] rattling about, and my children running around without shoes." Nevertheless, Jesús recognizes the problems his absence creates for his family. "It is very difficult to leave my children alone and not see them for almost a year," he says.

A Short-Term Active Migrant

Luis and Amelia López live with their seven children on the outskirts of Villanueva, the county seat of Villanueva municipio, a town of some 7,000 people. Their modest two-room home (a bedroom and a living room) can hardly hold all the family; both rooms double as playrooms, and the living room is not only for sleeping and playing but also for Luis to practice his trade, which is that of a tailor. It is good that they are young (Luis is 33 and Amelia, 31) because with their children (all under 13), their family business, and the necessity for Luis to work in the United States to make ends meet, the couple certainly have their hands full. Despite their location at the agricultural fringe of the city, the family lacks agricultural land. Luis had, as of 1987, made five trips to the United States, totaling three years of work.

Luis's father owned some land and was also a tailor. There were twelve children, of which Luis was the second. Although Luis wanted to continue studying and to become a cartoon artist or painter, he was forced to quit after primary school to help his father work the land. For a few months, he picked cotton in Los Mochis, Sinaloa. But the family was still so poor and so much in debt that Luis, at 21 (and just married), had to migrate to the United States in 1976 to look for work. Like many of his young friends, he chose Chicago as his destination, and paid a coyote $500 to get him there, without incident. In Chicago, his sisters-in-law helped him secure work in a garment factory, where he was able to put to use skills gained from his father. He was able to send home a maximum of $200 per month (living costs were high in Chicago), which his immediate family in Villanueva was able to use for food, clothing, a bed, and a few chairs for the home; and which his father was able to use for paying off the family debt. After a year and a half, Luis returned home to his wife and family, whom he missed very much.

Subsequent U.S. work trips, from 1980 on, were made not to Illinois but to California. The cost of arranging clandestine transportation to Chicago was much greater (over $500) than to California ($300). Furthermore, by this time Luis had several brothers in the Manhattan Beach and Redondo Beach areas of Los Angeles. In California, he worked initially in a restaurant before securing work in a garment plant. Living with relatives, by 1987 he was able to send as much as $350 per month home to his family. With this money, his father contracted masons in Villanueva to construct two new rooms on his house—a bedroom for his two daughters (aged 11 and 12), who "need their privacy," and a kitchen for Amelia.

A subsequent interview with this family was carried out upon a return visit to Villanueva in October 1989. Luis made two additional trips to the United States between January 1988, when he was first interviewed, and October 1989—both of them to Los Angeles, where he continued to live with family members. By this time, however, he had his own small tailor shop in Los Angeles. With the money he earned, his family was able to finish the kitchen and begin building a bathroom. But, despite the continued remittances sent home, Luis is trying to arrange for his immigration papers so that he can stay in Los Angeles, where his mother now lives. Amelia would like to stay in Villanueva, where she has always lived, but she is willing to join Luis in California, with all the children, if he is successful. Rosa, their eldest child (13 in 1989) expressed her strong desire to live in Los Angeles, where not only her father but her grandparents, aunts, uncles, and cousins live.

It is evident that Luis has mixed feelings about working in the United States. On the one hand, he has been able to add rooms to his home, and through his garment factory work in Los Angeles he has learned new cutting techniques that have bettered the quality of the pants he sews in his family business in Villanueva. His family earns an income of 5.7 million pesos per year ($4,070), over two million pesos higher than the average family in the town. On the other hand, as he puts it, "It is very sad to go [to the United States], and in my heart I could not go except for the necessity which obliges one to do such things." He has been apprehended and sent back twice; he has been cheated by a coyote; he has had to face very insensitive employers who refused to pay him. In addition, he notes, "My children respect me because they know that they should; but I have lost control of my family. . . . My family has begun to distance itself from me."

A Dormant Migrant

José Ramírez is a 35-year-old secondary school teacher who lives with his wife Graciela (37) in the city of Villanueva. They have four children aged 12, 8, 6, and 4. Theirs is a modest three-room home in a lower-middle-class barrio of the city. They own no land and no family businesses. Like some other Villanueva residents, José is not from the city itself but from a small community nearby—in José's case, Laguna del Carretero, off the main highway 15 kilometers to the south. José went once to the United States, sixteen years ago, where he worked for less than a month.

Interestingly, it was José's father, a farmer, who pushed him to go to school; the boy was not interested in studying. After primary school in Laguna del Carretero, his father arranged for him to enter secondary and later preparatory school in Rincón de Ramos, a city 30 kilometers north of Aguascalientes, where one of José's sisters lived. José returned to his parents' home, at 18, before completing preparatory school. There, he tried to fulfill his true aspiration, which was to work the land with his father.

It was in 1972, at 19, that José left his village with some friends to try his hand at work in the United States. It was not out of economic necessity, but to "find himself," that he made the trip. Crossing as mojados, he and his friends paid a coyote to transport them to Chicago. There José washed dishes in a restaurant. He was terrified of being caught and put in jail, however, and he found the society very "closed." His work in Chicago was just enough to cover his living expenses there. (It obviously pained

José to talk about this period of his life. In fact, when his wife was first surveyed she was unaware of the trip at all, because it happened before they were married and he evidently had never mentioned it.) José returned to Mexico after only two weeks in the United States, never to return.

The trip to the United States, however, marked a turning point in José's life. Returning to live in Aguascalientes, he met Graciela, and in anticipation of their marriage he began to look for work. With the level of education he had obtained, he was a good candidate for a teaching position, despite the fact he had never gone to a normal (teachers' preparation) school. He took a part-time job in Luis Moya, and after he and Graciela were married in 1974, he took successive jobs in Durango, Tacualeche, Sombrerete, and Villanueva, where he currently teaches. Motivated to increase his salary by his growing family, José moved his family to where the best job was to be found. He also upgraded his education by taking adult education classes. Despite his professional job, José barely makes it financially. His family income in 1987 was not quite 1.5 million pesos ($1,070 U.S.), 2 million pesos below the average for the city of Villanueva.

Undoubtedly influenced by his own experiences, José has a very negative view of U.S. migration. He notes that a large proportion of the migrants do not succeed economically in the United States. Furthermore, they often abandon their families or return with various vices regarding dress, language, and customs. In the schools, he sees many students who do not want to study because they are thinking of going to the United States and do not see the value of study. He also sees children who have gone to school in the United States, but who must repeat work in Mexico because their credits are not honored in Mexico. Among his neighbors who have gone, he sees a certain superiority complex—they feel that because they have dollars, they are better than other people.

José feels that the future of rural Mexico is to be found in two directions: investment by the government in agricultural credits and agricultural extension such as those under Echeverría; and the formation of small clothing enterprises such as those in Luis Moya. These will retain skilled labor locally and stop the deterioration of local values.

A Nonmigrant

Juan and Hermelinda Ojeda have their residence in the town of Luis Moya (population about 4,700 in 1987); however, the couple were separated in

1988 when the interviews were carried out—a rather sad example of economic and familial pressures. The couple have a daughter 3 years old and a son 15 days old; in addition, Hermelinda's 4-year-old son from a previous relationship lives with them. Their two-room home in Luis Moya lacks appliances of any sort, and furniture is minimal. The home does have electricity, but lacks drainage. Juan has never been to the United States.

Juan comes from a farming family of Pabellón, Aguascalientes, some 35 kilometers south of Luis Moya. The boy had wanderlust and a knack for doing many things—but not for studying. He quit school after three years and left home at 13. He married a woman while he was working in Jerez, but left her (and their children) after a few years. He was driving a gravel truck in Luis Moya in 1984 when he met and married Hermelinda, who is from Luis Moya. He was 25; she was 17. She already had a son (less than a year old) by a previous relationship. The father's family had sent the young man away to Mexico City; they refused to let him marry Hermelinda.

Shortly after Juan and Hermelinda were married, Juan began selling *paletas* (popsicles) from a cart in Luis Moya, visiting the small towns and farms nearby. This did not go well, because the work was seasonal, so Juan and Hermelinda decided in 1984 to go to Tijuana, where Hermelinda's sister resided. There, they lived with the sister, her husband, and another couple in a small house. Juan found work first in a tortilla factory, then tending pigs, and finally, repairing tires. But the family struggled because the pay was low and irregular, and it was impossible for someone with Juan's background to secure steady work in the northern Mexican metropolis. In 1985, the couple had a daughter in Tijuana. The family now had to support two young children. Juan began mistreating Hermelinda and her son. He also began to drink heavily. The couple separated in 1986, and she returned to Luis Moya to secure work in a tortilla factory, relying on her aunt and other family members to take care of her children. Juan came back to Luis Moya from time to time, but always returned to Tijuana, where he worked and lived with friends. Hermelinda and Juan had a new baby. Juan was invited by friends to travel to the United States to work, but, whether for lack of motivation or of money, he declined to do so.

Juan's case illustrates the underclass status of the poor nonmigrant group in Zacatecas. Juan and Hermelinda's joint income in Luis Moya in 1987 was only 1.3 million pesos ($930). Their case also illustrates the changing family lifestyles and economic distress of Mexico in the 1980s.

Northern Coahuila
A Long-Term Active Migrant

Encarnación Allende lives with his wife María del Carmen and their three children in their nicely furnished six-room home near downtown Morelos (1987 population, about 5,500), the county seat of Morelos municipio, at the heart of the fertile region known as the "five springs." The household boasts a truck and a telephone, the latter a relative rarity among Morelos households. Encarnación is a U.S. citizen, born in Poth, Texas, during a stay there by his mother. He is 39 years old and his wife is 35; their children are 12, 9, and 2 years of age. Although Encarnación gives his local occupation as "farmer" and owns 30 acres of irrigated land in Morelos, he rents the land out. His real occupation is groundskeeper at a golf course in San Antonio, Texas. He commutes to his home every two to eight weeks to see his family in Morelos. In all, Encarnación has cumulated more than five years of U.S. work experience.

Encarnación's parents dedicated themselves to agricultural work in Morelos. He was born during a difficult period in his parents' relationship, when they had separated and his mother had moved to Poth to be with her relatives. He was the youngest of six sons, and his parents saw to it that he finished secondary school. He married María when he was 25, in 1974, and despite his U.S. citizenship status, settled down to a farming life with his father and brothers, cultivating his land and raising a family in Morelos. His life was changed, however, by the death of his father in 1981. In order to pay for the funeral and cover other debts, he decided to move to San Antonio and to solicit help from family members in finding work there. At 32 years of age, Encarnación moved with his family to San Antonio, where they lived for six months while he worked as a golf course groundskeeper. He was able to earn $600 a month at this job.

María was not happy in the United States, and she returned to Morelos for good with her two children. She commented that during these six months in the United States, she felt estranged, rejected, and alone, and that "everyone lives in his or her own world, enclosed in their homes." Very aware of problems such as delinquency and drug addiction in the United States, she wanted her children to be educated in Morelos. Encarnación remained in San Antonio, sending home some $400 of his earnings each month. Since 1981, he has made dozens of visits to his family, either every other weekend or for longer periods of time every two months. His U.S. citizenship status has made it possible for him to continue this long-distance commuting pattern.

The Allende family's situation is atypical, but it does illustrate the legal status and the strong family and work ties with south Texas that many families of the region possess. María feels that the ability to provide well for his family has made her husband more responsible than he was before he went to the United States. He is committed to his family and to his community, and devotes all his time to them when he is in town. María comments that her family feels a certain distancing on the part of other families in the community who do not have U.S. workers. But the family is prospering economically and socially. Their income of more than 3 million pesos ($2,140) per year, along with appliances and goods that her husband brings back from the United States, enables them to live well in Morelos.

A Short-Term Active Migrant

David and Elva Villesca, like the Allendes, have a household whose head has been working off and on in the United States for the past several years. However, David, unlike Encarnación Allende, has no papers and must go away for longer periods of time to avoid the risk of multiple border crossings. The Villescas live in a three-room house in a lower-middle-class colonia at the periphery of the town of Morelos. David and Elva are both 32 years old, and they have six children aged 14 to 3. Their home has only a few modern conveniences—a television and stereo, but no drainage, no refrigerator or washing machine, no telephone, and no vehicles. David's profession is farming, but he has worked only intermittently at this in Morelos over the past ten years, having worked instead in the United States, where he has cumulated more than four years of work experience. Elva buys and resells clothing out of their home.

David comes from a large agricultural family that lives near Zaragoza, a town to the north of Morelos. The third of twelve children, he had to drop out of school after the third grade to help the family. David had a variety of abilities and worked as a butcher, as a cow milker, and at other farm-related jobs. After marrying in 1972 at the age of 16, David and his wife began to have children in quick succession—a daughter in 1974, sons in 1975 and 1977, another daughter in 1978. Realizing that he would not be able to support so many dependents without other sources of income, and acknowledging the success of a brother-in-law in Houston, he decided to set out for there. Crossing the border on foot, he made his way to Houston and took work assembling bicycles. Despite the fact that he lived with his in-laws, he was able to send home only $100–$140 each month, owing to his low wages at this job. He returned to Morelos in 1980, but worked irregularly there.

By 1983, he found himself in difficult economic straits again and decided to migrate to Dallas where his paternal uncle and his cousins lived. He crossed by foot, and to avoid being apprehended, walked through the brush country for a week, eating nopales, until he reached a city outside of the border zone. In Dallas, with the help of his cousins he found good work—first as a milkman, then as a plumber by day and bank janitor by night. He was able to send home $200 per month. The plumbing job has proved a lasting one, and he has returned to it several times after visits home. The family's income of 3.3 million pesos (some $2,400) is adequate for most of their needs. When his wife was interviewed in late April of 1987, David had been in the United States for four months.

David's extended absences have caused suffering for his family. His wife feels that this affects the children, who have lost respect for their father. But it also affects her; she feels alone and unprotected in Morelos. She does not acknowledge her loneliness to her neighbors, for fear of being taken advantage of by them. David is now attempting to establish residency in the United States, in order to get amnesty; thus, he must stay there continuously until his status is determined. If David is granted resident status, she acknowledges that the family would move there, which would be better for them because they would be better off economically and they would be together.

A Dormant Migrant

Pedro Gómez illustrates a certain type of U.S. migrant from the border region who crosses extensively before settling down in Mexico. Pedro is unusual in that these work experiences occupied the first 42 years of his life, during which he never married. He married his wife Guadalupe in 1983; he was 44 and she was 16. The couple has three children aged 6, 3, and 1. Their home, in a lower-middle-class barrio in the town of Morelos, has three rooms, with minimal conveniences—there is a refrigerator and a television, but no drainage, washing machine, or household vehicle. Pedro works as a night watchman at the large thermoelectric plant near the town of Nava, a few miles east of Morelos.

Pedro's early agricultural background resembles that of many other men of the area, but Pedro's family had no land—his father was a farm laborer. As the oldest of three children, he had to quit school at 11 years of age (after fourth grade) to help the family. He worked in agriculture with his father and had no future aspirations for himself. However, at 15 he joined a group of friends who crossed the Rio Grande in 1953, as much for adventure as work. After walking across the countryside for several days, he took up work putting in fences on a ranch in Ozuna, Texas. Because he was paid so little ($45 per month) he was able to send home only $350 over eight months, despite the fact that the rancher provided his room and board. But the money was of great use to his family, providing meals and clothing for his brother and sister in Morelos.

Over the next 18 years, Pedro returned to the United States some 60 times. He worked in many cities and towns in Texas—Sonora, Carrizo Springs, Corpus Christi, San Antonio—in diverse jobs including ranch work, harvesting crops, and construction. He was apprehended more than ten times by the U.S. Immigration and Naturalization Service, but returned soon after each deportation, always to a different location. At first he sent home as much money as possible. Then Pedro began drinking heavily, and for a period of several years he sent very little money home. During his last two years working in the United States (1979–81), seeing his father become feebler and less able to work, Pedro renounced his drinking and worked continuously at his job in construction in San Antonio. With the $2,200 he was able to send home, his family was able to construct a larger home. Pedro was then 42 years old.

Pedro's life changed greatly upon the death of his father in 1981. He returned to Morelos to become the head of his household. Soon afterward (1983), he married Guadalupe, and at last started a household and family of his own. Since 1983 he has not returned to the United States. He does not want to leave his young family alone. In addition, he considers it difficult to find work in the United States with the passage of the Immigration Reform and Control Act (and he doesn't qualify for amnesty under the provisions of the law). From his job as night watchman at the thermoelectric plant, Pedro's family income in 1987 was 1.6 million pesos (about $1,150)—barely enough to get by. He views his hometown as very backward compared to the United States, and he recalls the importance of U.S. dollars to his family. However, he also recalls the difficulties of life in the United States—the arduous crossings and apprehensions and the long searches for work; the threats to his life from bandits, coyotes, local workers at the destinations, and other migrants; and the loneliness of life without his family.

A Nonmigrant

Tomás and Maricarmen Villaseñor live in the mining and manufacturing city of Nueva Rosita, which had a population of around 35,000 in 1987. They are 48 and 42 years old, respectively, and have four children aged 8 to 19. Tomás's father (80) and mother (75) both live with the family as well. Their home, in a middle-class barrio of the city, is a modest four-room cement-block house with internal drainage. The family, atypically, does not have a television set. Tomás is a coal miner in the nearby Esperanzas mine; his wife is a cleaning woman at a primary school in the city. Neither has been to the United States to work, nor to any other city in Mexico to work.

Tomás is from a large working-class family of Sabinas, Coahuila, which is Nueva Rosita's "twin city" of some 43,000, only a couple of miles away. His family moved to Nueva Rosita when Tomás was only 3 years old. He was able to complete primary school, but then had to begin working. He was married to Maricarmen at 27 years of age, in 1967. The Villaseñors' family income was only 1.8 million pesos in 1987—some $1,300. Occasionally one of Tomás's brothers who works in the United States sends some money home to his parents. This is minimal, however—only $10 in 1987, for example.

The Villaseñors see many disadvantages from U.S. migration, principal among them the effect of the father's absence on the children. The wife "is left alone to battle with the problems." Without the cementing effect of family unity, the children go astray. They get involved with the wrong group of people. They lack discipline and order in their lives, which the father provides.

6

Migration and the Economic Base of Central Zacatecas

The importance of U.S. migration at the family level in central Zacatecas invites the question of what its role is at the community and regional levels. A community's economic condition is not just the summation of the economic condition of all its households. Such a summation would ignore the condition of businesses and other establishments in the community, as well as the linkages between households and businesses in the larger region and beyond that help to determine that condition.

Because it brings in money from outside the community, migration is a basic activity; but it is not the only, or necessarily the most important, such activity in this region. Zacatecas is a state undergoing rapid economic change. By the late 1980s it had many new commercial agricultural operations and private industries producing for export to other regions and to the United States. Some of these activities were located in the study municipios; others were located in nearby cities such as Zacatecas or Fresnillo, where they were already drawing commuters from the study municipios. In this chapter we compare the roles of different basic sectors, including migration, in towns across the region. We also attempt to predict how further trade liberalization under the North American Free Trade Agreement (NAFTA) will affect incomes and migration across these towns. The Zacatecas sample covers a large enough number of towns to make such a comparative analysis at the town level possible, but the Coahuila sample does not. Therefore, unfortunately, no economic base analysis of Coahuila is included here.

Past research on villages in rural west-central Mexico has argued that neither Mexican government policy nor U.S. migration has been able to develop the region, and in fact that both have contributed to its stagnation. This literature tends to be pessimistic, concluding that without U.S. migration the region suffers, and that with it, it also suffers. Moreover, there is little optimism that substitutes for U.S. migration can be found that will

110

make such migration unnecessary, at least in the short run. In a recent book, the authors and editors generally conclude that no economic alternatives to migration in this region look really promising, whether they entail government agricultural programs, small private businesses, small-scale industry, or commuting to industrial jobs in nearby metropolises (Díaz-Briquets and Weintraub 1991).

The previous chapters present a somewhat more positive view on the role of U.S. migration in family economic advancement. The present chapter presents a more optimistic view of the growth-generating potential of some of the other basic sectors in the entire central Zacatecas region, based on economic base analyses and case studies in the study municipios.

Economic Base Methodology

The economic base technique has a terminology all its own, and its proper application involves carefully following a series of analytical steps that can be confusing to the uninitiated. I present this terminology and these steps here so that the "initiated" will understand the definitions used and the assumptions made in applying the technique to my data. The general reader may well decide to skip this section and move right to the results.

As discussed briefly in chapter 1, the community economic base technique provides a framework for analyzing the multiplier effects of different basic sectors on income and employment growth in a community (Tiebout 1962; Weiss and Gooding 1968; Garrison 1972; Jones 1991). Initially, the technique requires defining the boundaries of the community and then separating internal (nonbasic) from external (basic) demand for all the goods and services offered by that community. Here, we use *internal* to refer to the urbanized or built-up area of a particular town, and *external* to mean everywhere outside of this area. Next, basic and nonbasic amounts (of either income or employment) are calculated for each major economic sector in the town, and the town's total income or employment is calculated. In order to determine the independent multiplier effects (on total income or employment) for each basic sector, the researcher applies multiple-regression analysis either to time-series data for a given community or to spatial data for a number of communities at a given point in time. The latter procedure is followed here.

Information from various studies suggests that six economic sectors account for most of the basic or external income in communities of rural central Mexico: (1) U.S. migration; (2) internal migration; (3) commuting to nearby cities; (4) commercial agriculture; (5) private businesses (clothing and furniture stores, medical practices, banks, manufacturing plants, etc.); and (6) government (federal and state agencies, schools and hospitals, etc.). Transfer payments (for example, government support payments for families) are not significant in central Mexico—in contrast to their importance in rural areas of the United States (see Garrison 1972). The above six sectors are therefore the ones explicitly considered for central Zacatecas.

Data on basic income by town were obtained from the establishment questionnaire mentioned briefly in chapter 1 (appendix C). Private businesses, government agencies, and nonprofit organizations (e.g., the Catholic Church) were all included under the term *establishments*. A total of 136 establishments in five towns—the five largest towns in the three municipios—were interviewed. These towns contained the great majority of all the establishments in the survey region. Their names and the numbers of establishments interviewed were as follows: Villanueva (in Villanueva municipio), 49 interviews; Jerez (Jerez), 36; Luis Moya (Luis Moya), 28; Tayahua (Villanueva), 12; and Malpaso (Villanueva), 11.

Prior to the interviews, a complete list of all town establishments by size was obtained from a combination of sources including the local tax rolls, interviews with the municipal president, and local telephone directories. Then, in each town, all of the largest establishments were targeted for interviewing, plus a random sample of the smaller establishments, stratified by subtype (there were nine specific subtypes and a miscellaneous category). As with the household questionnaires, the establishment questionnaires were administered by two-person interview teams. The questionnaire itself was two pages long, and included questions on the products or services and number of local employees of the establishment; the approximate sales or budget, and the percentage of the sales or budget deriving from outside sources in 1987; the migratory history of the business manager or owner; the approximate amount and source of purchased factors of production, including labor, in 1987; and the manager or owner's opinions on what would be needed to develop the local economy. The average interview required about 15 minutes.

Arrival at estimates of each town's economic base involved a necessarily complex procedure. Simply put, the procedure was to use household questionnaire data, including the locations where household members worked, to attribute each household's income to basic and nonbasic sources within each of the six above economic sectors. Establishment income was then parceled into basic and nonbasic components for the same six sectors based on data on local versus external sales (or funding sources, in the case of nonprofit establishments) from the establishment questionnaire. Procedures were employed to ensure that household and establishment income were not double-counted (e.g, in the case of family businesses). Finally, sampling ratios were applied to both household and establishment figures, in order to estimate the sectoral and total income for the total population of establishments and households in the town. The smaller towns of Tayahua and Malpaso were used to estimate basic proportions for establishment income in the small towns where no establishment interviews were carried out.

For each household the following portions of local income were recorded as basic income: (1) all U.S. migrant earnings; (2) all earnings from internal migration; (3) all income earned by household members who worked daily in nearby towns and cities (commuting income); (4) agricultural income from the sales of products outside the town; (5) private business income from sales to, or services rendered to, outlying customers; (6) federal and state government payrolls, and the proportion of local government payrolls met from outside funds.

The result of these procedures was a set of characteristics—total income and basic income per capita for each of the six above sectors—for a total of 22 towns in central Zacatecas. Demographic data on each town, from the 1990 Mexican census—including population, labor force structure, and distances to nearby cities—were added to the data set to serve as statistical controls. The 22 towns with their sizes, sample sizes, and average household incomes appear in table 6.1.

An Overview of the Region's Economic Base

Considering the region as a whole, U.S. migrant remittances bring in more money from outside (44 percent of the total) than any other sector (table 6.2, basic income column). In second and third places are private business and agriculture (with 21 and 16 percent, respectively). Thus, these typically Mexican communities, with their adobe architecture and corn-and-beans agriculture, beneath the surface are heavily supported by U.S. migrant remittances from hundreds and thousands of miles away. This is not unexpected; all the previous chapters have suggested it. What is important to note, however, is that just because a sector earns the most

Table 6.1 Towns Included in the Economic Base Analysis

Town	Abbreviations for Graphs in Fig. 6.1	Municipio	Estimated Population 1987	No. of Households Surveyed	Mean HH Income, 1987, in 1,000 Pesos
1. Villanueva	VI	Villanueva	7,290	109	3,750
2. Tayahua	TA	"	3,180	50	2,697
3. Malpaso	MP	"	3,140	40	2,497
4. Felipe Angeles	FA	"	1,510	24	2,620
5. Boca de Rivera	BR	"	740	10	3,330
6. Francisco Murguía	FM	"	810	9	2,188
7. La Encarnación	LE	"	1,170	15	4,830
8. El Tigre	ET	"	850	12	1,566
9. La Quemada	LQ	"	970	12	3,756
10. S. Tadeo de las Flores	ST	"	280	6	2,017
11. Emiliano Zapata	EZ	"	360	9	3,032
12. Tenango	TE	"	270	6	3,765
13. Luis Moya	LM	Luis Moya	4,660	61	3,657
14. Esteban Castorena	EC	"	970	18	2,529
15. La Noria de Molinos	NM	"	740	15	3,525
16. Jerez	JE	Jerez	29,660	99	4,279
17. Ermita Guadalupe	EG	"	3,000	18	6,895
18. Luis Moya	LMJ	"	1,010	7	3,767
19. Cargadero	CA	"	830	18	7,452
20. Los Murillo	MU	"	250	8	3,788
21. Los Haros	LH	"	1,140	16	7,422
22. Benito Juárez	BJ	"	320	6	2,342

external income does not mean it necessarily has the highest multiplier effect on local growth, as will be seen shortly.

Job commuting accounts for a surprisingly large 13 percent of basic income in the region. Much of this income is earned by residents of small towns traveling to larger towns and cities within 50 kilometers. For example, residents of El Tigre and San Tadeo work in adjacent Villanueva; those in Cargadero and Ermita Guadalupe work in Jerez; those in Malpaso work in Jerez and Zacatecas (see fig. 2.2). Evidently, commuting in this region is more important than in other central Mexican towns (Cornelius 1990, 122). However, commuting is not nearly as important for metropolitan-adjacent towns in Mexico as for such towns in the United States; for example, two small towns in south Texas that are 20–30 miles from San Antonio earn around 60 percent of job income from commuting to that city (Jones 1987, 1990). This underlines the much greater mobility of Texan as opposed to Zacatecan workers.

Internal migrant remittances are unimportant, accounting for less than

Table 6.2 Sectoral Components of Total and Basic Income per Household:
Central Zacatecas

	All Places		Urban Places		Rural Places	
	Total	Basic	Total	Basic	Total	Basic
Avg. HH income (1,000 pesos)	3,945	2,631	4,005	2,846	3,913	2,517
% Distribution of income by economic sector:						
External jobs:						
U.S. migrant remittances	29.4	44.1	24.4	34.3	32.2	50.0
Internal migrant remits.	.6	.9	.7	1.0	.6	.9
Job commuting income	8.5	12.7	7.4	10.4	9.0	14.1
Local jobs:						
Agricultural sector	33.4	16.2	14.8	6.0	43.5	22.3
Private business sector	24.0	20.9	46.5	40.5	11.7	9.0
Government sector (L, S, N)	3.1	4.3	5.5	7.0	1.8	2.6
Other sources[a]	1.0	(1.0)[b]	.7	(.7)[b]	1.2	(1.2)[b]
Total	100.0	100.1	100.0	99.9	100.0	100.1
Number of HHs sampled	585	585	204	204	381	381

a. Pensions, rent, interest, etc.
b. The basic component of "other sources" is unknown. To allow comparison of the total
and basic income distributions, it is assumed that these sources are basic to the same degree as the average for all other sectors.

1 percent of basic income. This supports research cited earlier, which noted
that migration-prone regions tend to send either international migrants or
internal migrants, but not both (Zazueta and Corona 1979).

The dominance of U.S. migrant earnings is strongest for rural places,
accounting for one-half of basic income there; but even in the urban places
(Jerez and Villanueva) these migrant earnings account for more than one-
third of income (table 6.2). In the urban places, the private business sector,
accounting for over 40 percent of basic income, is somewhat more important than U.S. migration. Note that commuting to work outside of the
locality constitutes 14 percent of the basic income for rural places, versus
10 percent for urban places. The 14 percent figure for rural places is not
insignificant. In fact, commuting is the third-largest basic income source
in rural areas, ahead of private businesses, government, and internal migration. Considering the current entry of large export-oriented firms into central Zacatecas, the propensity to commute may be important for these rural
municipios, potentially enabling them to benefit from the industrial development in nearby cities. Furthermore, with better transportation, this propensity could in time increase.

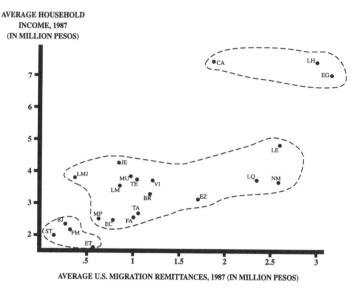

AVERAGE HOUSEHOLD
INCOME, 1987
(IN MILLION PESOS)

AVERAGE U.S. MIGRATION REMITTANCES, 1987 (IN MILLION PESOS)

Figure 6.1a Relationship between remittances and household income in towns of central Zacatecas, 1987 (see table 6.1 for abbreviated names)

Impacts of Basic Income Sources on Town Income

Towns that have high migrant remittances tend to have high household incomes (fig. 6.1a). This relationship is a linear one (r_p = .738, a strong positive correlation). The trend shown on the graph can be broken down into three clusters of points. First, in the upper right, are three small "U.S.-dependent" centers, with high remittances and high incomes. This cluster includes the towns of Cargadero, Ermita Guadalupe, and Los Haros, all in Jerez, where heavy U.S. migration rates have resulted in high incomes owing to extensive investments in commercial agriculture. Second, in the middle, are large and medium-sized "U.S.-oriented" towns and urban areas such as Jerez, Villanueva, Malpaso, and Tayahua, with moderate remittances and moderate incomes. These places have more diversified economies including significant business earnings. Third, there are the small "tributary" communities near a county seat, such as El Tigre and San Tadeo de las Flores near Villanueva, or Benito Juárez near Jerez, with low U.S. remittances and low incomes. These small towns are dependent on jobs in nearby cities and, occasionally, elsewhere in Mexico. Their residents eke out an existence, taking low-paying, low-status urban jobs.

Towns that have high levels of commercial agriculture (external sales of agricultural products) also tend to have high household incomes (fig. 6.1b). This strong relationship ($r_p = .742$) is based upon a few commercial agricultural centers where innovative farmers have geared up to meet the demands of a national market. The graph indicates that two points—the towns of Los Haros and Cargadero—have both large commercial agricultural investments and large incomes. The high figures for these places are not a fluke; they are based on a substantial number of families, each of whom had large agricultural investments. There were 16 and 18 family interviews in these towns, respectively. This graph, although "pulled" toward Los Haros and Cargadero, also illustrates a continuum of sorts—from the commercial peach-growing centers of Los Haros and Cargadero; to the grape, grain, and feed cattle towns of Luis Moya and Los Murillo; to the other towns, which include both the moderate-income larger towns and cities and the small, poor towns of Villanueva municipio with their subsistence corn-and-beans production and their tributary relationships to the larger towns and cities.

These graphs suggest that migrant remittances and commercial agriculture are both responsible for the region's income growth, and that both

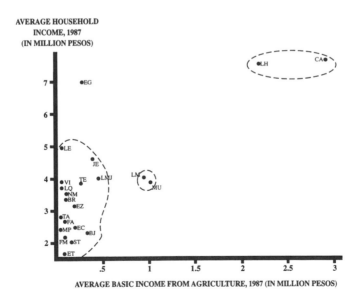

Figure 6.1b Relationship between commercial agriculture and household income in towns of central Zacatecas, 1987 (see table 6.1 for abbreviated names)

will play a role in the future. The definitive proof of this comes from a multiple-regression analysis, in which the six basic sources are considered simultaneously in relation to household income. Initial analyses indicated that only three of the six sectors—U.S. migrant remittances, (commercial) agriculture, and private business—played a significant role, through the multiplier mechanism, in the growth of local income. Other sectors— internal migration, commuting, and government jobs—played a minor role (they tended to be significant only for the poorest places, where no other alternatives existed, and they did not lead to income growth). These three were not considered further.

The results show that a town's commercial agriculture sector may have a greater impact, per peso earned, than the town's U.S. migration sector—despite the fact that U.S. migration accounts for much more income. Average household income (y) is a function of U.S. remittances (u), agricultural jobs (a), and private business jobs (b), as follows:

$$y = 1,582 + 1.08u + 1.34a + 1.01b \, (R^2 = .893)$$

The first number (1,582), the intercept of the function, is the average number of pesos (in thousands) a family in the town would earn if each of these three sources of basic income yielded zero—that is, if the town had to do without them entirely (relying on the three minor sectors and whatever other sources there happened to be). The numerical coefficients for the sources are the income multipliers, reflecting the number of pesos by which household income would increase in the town per one-peso increase in the particular basic income source, controlling for all of the other sources. Note that the highest multiplier for basic investment in the region is for agriculture, not for U.S. migration. In monetary terms, for each 100 pesos of commercial agricultural products that the farmers of a town sell outside of town, the total income of the town increases by 134 pesos—the original 100 pesos, plus 34 pesos that are recycled within the local economy due to the fact that the farmers do some shopping locally, and that local shop owners do some shopping locally, and so on, completing the cycle. For U.S. migration, each 100 pesos of remittances generates only an additional 8 pesos through local income recycling, and for private businesses, only an additional 1 peso.

None of these figures is high, as multipliers go, and they are subject to the various assumptions of this analysis. Nevertheless, at a minimum we can say that in central Zacatecas the development of commercial agriculture creates more productive linkages within the region than does U.S.

migration. (This statement must be qualified, though, because past U.S. remittances may have been invested in commercial agriculture, resulting in higher incomes; U.S. remittances may have thereby played an indirect role in the development of other sectors.) It is not possible, with the available data, to trace out these linkages over time. However, detailed interviews in Jerez municipio do provide evidence for them.

Interestingly, the statistical relationship between U.S. migrant remittances and basic income from agriculture is positive ($r_p = +.299$). This suggests that U.S. migration and commercial agriculture are supplementary to each other, rather than complementary (otherwise, the sign would be negative). That is, U.S. migration appears to help support commercial agriculture (and vice versa), rather than replacing it. If so, then the argument that increasing trade liberalization (including considerable agribusiness investment) will lead to decreasing migration from the area may not be valid.

Case Studies: Commercial Agriculture in Central Zacatecas

We now turn to several case studies which illustrate how commercial agriculture has developed in central Zacatecas in recent years. In the period from 1988 to the present, many municipios in Zacatecas, including rural and isolated ones, have benefited directly from productive investments in commercial agriculture. In the cases of Jerez and Luis Moya, past U.S. migration has been the source of the funds for some of these investments. In some cases, the financial success of the investment ventures has obviated the need for further U.S. migration.

Peaches in Jerez Municipio

The most dramatic example of locally initiated economic development in the whole region is the peach orchards of Jerez (see map, fig. 2.2). The peach zone lies to the north of Jerez city, on the slopes of the Sierra Madres Occidentales between 7,000 and 10,000 feet (2,134–3,048 m). Before 1965 this region was grain and cattle country. In the early 1960s, a local farmer from Cargadero by the name of Jesús Saldivar Valdez, who had worked as a bracero in the peach orchards of California's Central Valley, returned with peach seedlings and the knowledge of how to raise them. His successful plantings led to many other local farmers' following suit, and by 1988 the municipio of Jerez boasted some 20,000 hectares

(50,800 acres) of orchards. Continued migration to the Central Valley after the bracero period reinforced local farmers' techniques, and they became efficient at creating nurseries, transplanting, pruning, and harvesting.
Just as important, growers began to contract with middlemen to deliver
their fruit to major urban markets such as Mexico City and Guadalajara.
The local growers claim that their fruit, small and hard, has a distinctive,
tart flavor and is superior to peaches raised anywhere else in the country.

The initial developments were almost entirely initiated and financed by
individual growers, particularly in the Cargadero area, where most production is on small private plots of between 5 and 20 acres. In the past ten
years, the federal government has gotten involved, through its SARH (Agriculture and Water Ministry) and CONAFRUT (National Fruit Commis-
sion) offices in Jerez. These offices have undertaken several projects on local *ejidos* (collective farms) such as Los Haros and El Durazno, including
construction of three peach-selection plants, plans for a processing plant,
technical advice on increasing yields, cooperative marketing arrangements
to cut out the high costs of middlemen, and the organization of local pro-
ducers into their own peach growers' association. The government became
interested when it saw that the private initiatives were proving successful.
Since then, government-financed operations have more than matched the
acreage, productivity, and quality of peaches produced by the private
growers.

From the present perspective of alternatives to U.S. migration, the most
interesting aspects of peach production in the region are that this production was initially financed by migrant remittances (and engineered with
knowledge gained in the United States) and that its financial success has
enabled many farmers to forgo U.S. migration (in fact, they have had to
forgo it in order to take adequate care of their trees during seeding, pruning, and harvesting, which span the months of February to October).

But most importantly, peaches are a new force in local economic development. High levels of investment in land, machinery, chemicals, and labor
are occurring in a region that has traditionally had one of the highest U.S.
emigration rates in the country. Assuming that future U.S. migration is
curtailed by a combination of U.S. immigration policy and the difficulty of
finding jobs in the United States, peach production will be an attractive
alternative for the households of the region. It is labor intensive, has linkages to other sectors of the regional economy (e.g., the packing and processing industry, the agricultural chemicals and machinery industries, and
the transportation sector), is potentially adaptable to some of the poorer

municipios of the state (e.g., Villanueva), and has the potential for eventual exports to the United States.

Wine in Luis Moya Municipio

Wine production in Zacatecas dates from the colonial period. However, its modern period of growth began in the late 1960s. Stimulated by the success of grape production and processing in Aguascalientes and Coahuila, grape acreage in the state nearly doubled, to some 7,000 hectares (almost 18,000 acres), between 1970 and 1980. Studies indicate that grapes yield more gross income per acre than any other crop in the state (Secretaria de Agricultura y Recursos Hidráulicos 1982, 265).

The physical environment in central Zacatecas is excellent for grapes. Two major grape-growing zones exist—one around Fresnillo (north of Zacatecas), where ejido production predominates; and the other centered on Luis Moya (to the south) where private production, both small and large scale, is found (fig. 2.2). In the former case, the government is actively involved with financing and assisting the *ejidatarios*. Thus grapes, just like peaches, illustrate initiatives by both the public and private sectors within the state. In the municipio of Luis Moya, on alluvial soils at the eastern base of the Sierra Fría mountains, the physical conditions are especially suitable. Subterranean water upwells in springs to provide irrigation, which is essential for high quality grapes. Gently sloping land and cool temperatures are helpful, although the elevation (6,200 feet at the cabecera) can bring occasional damaging frosts. Highway access to market is good.

In Luis Moya, grapes are over 90 percent "industrial"—that is, grown for processing into table wines and into distilled spirits that are shipped elsewhere for making brandy. Grape production was given a great stimulus during the 1970s, with the establishment of a number of local wine and spirit plants in Luis Moya. The largest is Vides, S.A., established in 1977, located between Luis Moya and Ojocaliente. This plant hired 47 full-time workers in 1988, and several times that during the harvest from June to November. Most of these workers were from the municipios of Luis Moya and Ojocaliente, especially from ranchos and other rural localities. The plant's principal product is the distilled spirit called *aguardiente*, which is shipped to the state of Mexico to make the famous Pedro Domeq brandy. Like the many smaller plants within the municipio, Vides produces for the domestic rather than the international market.

The production of grapes would seem to present an attractive alternative to U.S. migration for several of the poorer municipios of southern Zacatecas, which are sending large numbers of migrants to the United States. These municipios have some of the physical (if not the economic) prerequisites for production—gently sloping lands with a cool climate and subsurface water supply, and access to markets in Zacatecas and Guadalajara. Villanueva and the area farther into the mountainous "right foot" of the state (the canyon of Juchipila) would seem especially appropriate. In fact, in northernmost Villanueva municipio, acreages of grapes have already been planted and are beginning to yield returns.

Broccoli in Luis Moya Municipio

Another commercial product—broccoli—is being produced in several municipios in the vicinity of the city of Zacatecas, including Villa de Cos, Loreto, Ojocaliente, and Luis Moya. These municipios do not tend to have such high levels of U.S. migration as Jerez or Villanueva, because they lie on flat land irrigated with wells, in the well-served "industrial corridor" stretching from north of Zacatecas to north of Aguascalientes. Broccoli production provides one more migration alternative in a portfolio of alternatives (vegetables, grapes, apparel) that have existed in the region for over 20 years. As with peach production in Jerez and wine production in Luis Moya, broccoli in Luis Moya illustrates the relatively high returns on commercial agricultural investment. Broccoli, however, has an additional attribute not found with peaches or grapes—its orientation to the international market, through transnational corporations that have recently opened labor-intensive operations in the municipio.

Broccoli production in central Zacatecas was begun in the early 1980s by a farmer named Rodolfo Ibarra in Loreto municipio east of Luis Moya. From the start, the market was principally foreign—the most important consumers are frozen food companies in the United States. The idea spread to Ibarra's brothers, and to many other farmers in Loreto. Soon, many municipios of central Zacatecas, from Villa de Cos, north of Zacatecas, to Loreto to the south, were producing broccoli, over 85 percent of it for export. At the beginning, farmers in the region were contracted by processing plants in Aguascalientes, which then shipped the broccoli frozen for final packaging in the United States. In the mid-1980s, the Mexican firm of La Huerta (or, as it is called locally, "Medio Kilo") opened a processing plant in Ojocaliente, contracting workers in the Loreto and Ojocaliente areas to produce broccoli for them, destined for the U.S. market.

Stimulated by the success of La Huerta, Stokeley's, Inc., (whose home office is in Wisconsin) built a processing plant just outside of Luis Moya in 1990. This plant benefited from the existing know-how of farmers who were already supplying La Huerta, from the ready supply of workers in the immediate vicinity, and from its central location relative to other broccoli-producing districts in the Bajío and in Durango and southern Coahuila. The plant cuts, washes, precooks, freezes, and boxes the broccoli for shipment to its packaging plant in Wisconsin. Stokeley's also operates processing plants in Aguascalientes and in the Bajío of Guanajuato.

The Stokeley's plant was in 1992 the largest single employer in Luis Moya, hiring 450 workers (75 percent women) in the plant itself, in addition to some 100 producing farmers with whom contracts are worked out. Thus, the plant has had a significant impact on economic development in a municipio that already was producing wine and apparel for shipment to major cities in Mexico.

Since plant employees rarely come from farther than 20 kilometers to work at the plant, employment benefits from Stokeley's have not diffused to poorer, emigrant municipios such as Villa Gonzalez or Villanueva, both of which lie more than 50 kilometers away. Furthermore, farmers in these latter municipios lack experience in commercial agriculture, so that large companies could not rely upon broccoli from there unless they were willing to train and provision the farmers. Nevertheless, these poorer municipios do have some of the prerequisites—accessibility, flat land, a temperate climate, and a surplus labor supply—that might make the future entry of commercial vegetable production successful. Twenty-five years ago, Luis Moya had little commercial agriculture. Today, however, the municipio is a dynamic agribusiness center. This turnabout offers some hope for the future of today's emigrant municipios of central Zacatecas.

Conclusions

Díez-Canedo (1984, 60–61), using data on U.S. postal money orders deposited in Mexican banks, identified Zacatecas as the Mexican state with the highest per capita U.S. remittances. These remittances accounted for almost two-thirds of the gross territorial product of the state in the mid-1970s. The results of the research presented here suggest that U.S.

earnings are high, but not as dominant as they appeared in Díez-Canedo's research. In central Zacatecas, in order of importance, agriculture, U.S. migrant remittances, and private business each accounted for between one-third and one-fourth of total income in the towns studied.

However, if we consider basic income—income generated by demand outside of the town—then U.S. migration stands out much more. The reason for this is that all U.S. earnings are external, in contrast to those from agriculture and private business, some of which derive from within the town. U.S. migration accounted for 44 percent of basic income; followed by private businesses and agriculture, with less than half that figure; and commuting to external jobs in cities, which accounted for considerably less than a third. Neither internal migration nor government was important. U.S. migration was more important for rural than for urban places, accounting for half of the basic income in the former and one-third in the latter.

Examination of individual towns in the region reveals that household incomes are a function of two factors: U.S. migrant remittances and investments in commercial agriculture. Furthermore, the multiplier for agricultural income is higher than that for U.S. migrant remittances.

The latter conclusion suggests that agribusinesses now in operation in particular municipios in central Zacatecas might be successfully introduced into municipios in the region that have had little such investment, and which currently depend heavily on U.S. migration. Case studies of peach production in Jerez, and both wine and broccoli production in Luis Moya, show that these ventures have resulted in increased employment and income in towns that in the past depended more on U.S. migration. In Jerez, migrant remittances are being reinvested in new peach orchards, in some cases obviating the necessity for further U.S. migration.

Further analysis suggests that the ability of these types of ventures to succeed in other towns depends on two factors: the degree to which the physical environment and the location's accessibility are similar to those in the "successful" towns; and the degree to which the towns' demographic characteristics—population size, labor force structure, educational level, and so forth—are similar to those of the successful towns. In central Zacatecas, one of the curious facts is that towns in adjacent municipios are vastly different from each other in levels of economic advancement despite being so similar in physical and demographic characteristics (other than income). This is most evident when we compare towns in Jerez and Luis Moya municipios, on the one hand, with towns in Villanueva on the other.

All Villanueva seems to lack are the investments themselves and the political will and entrepreneurship to make them work.

These hypothetical results are fraught with many assumptions, but one point seems undeniable: that further investment in commercial agriculture is desirable for central Zacatecas. This strategy capitalizes on strong economic multipliers due to agriculture's linkages to other local sectors. It builds on past successes in adjacent towns and municipios. It is in line with the competitive advantage Mexico is expected to enjoy in horticultural specialties under the terms of NAFTA. Finally, under certain conditions, it has the potential in the long run to lower U.S. migration rates. Today, U.S. remittances boost productive investments; later on, if these investments bear fruit, U.S. migration will be less necessary and might decline.

7

Conclusions and Further Research Questions

The structural or dependency perspective argues that U.S. migration leads to dependency, disinvestment, inequality, and the disintegration of local institutions. It is based on "village" studies by anthropologists and sociologists, particularly studies carried out prior to the early 1980s. The functionalist perspective, which draws positive conclusions about the effects of U.S. migration—greater economic security, reinvestment, a lessening of income differentials, and the strengthening of family and community ties—tends to be based on studies at higher spatial levels of analysis (regional and national), often done by economists, and published since the mid-1980s.

This book attempts to enlighten some of these disagreements. To a significant degree, they can be traced to the scale of the studies, the stage of migration at which the towns in question find themselves, and the geographic regions in which the towns are located. In looking at U.S. migration in north-central Mexico, I have endeavored to examine its impacts at family as well as town and regional scales; to examine these impacts for various stages of the migration process; and to compare two subregions—central Zacatecas and northern Coahuila—separated by four hundred miles as well as by major physical and historical differences.

A grant from the National Science Foundation (#SES-8619504) made it possible to carry out a detailed questionnaire survey of 596 nonmetropolitan households in central Zacatecas and 466 in nonmetropolitan northern Coahuila, during the spring and early summer of 1988. The five municipios were chosen on the basis of their high rates of undocumented U.S. migration and their relative proximity to metropolitan areas. Within the municipios, towns and villages for interviewing were chosen by size and location using a random procedure, with the ratio of rural to urban households adhering to the rural/urban ratio from the 1980 Mexican census for

126

each subregion. Three interview teams of two members each administered a four-page household interview schedule to families selected randomly from each town. In addition to these schedules, more detailed follow-up interviews were carried out in person with 20 households in the two regions. Also, an establishment interview schedule was completed for 271 businesses, nonprofit organizations, and offices for use in the regional impact analyses.

Historical Forces

A careful reading of the Spanish- and English-language literature uncovers political and economic forces that have through recent history shaped the situation of both central Zacatecas and northern Coahuila, and provides clues to the widespread U.S. migration from both regions.

Central Zacatecas has had a difficult history; its economic structure was ravaged by opposing armies in the independence and revolutionary periods, and its land controlled by *hacendados* (large landholders) in between. It has always been an area of subsistence beans-and-corn agriculture, cattle grazing, and silver mining. U.S. migration established itself in the late 1800s, and accelerated with the Mexican Revolution, the bracero program, and then the Mexican economic crisis of the 1980s. The physical environment is not really a determining factor in the underdevelopment of the region: other cool, semiarid steppe regions with similar environmental conditions are productive in cattle grazing, forestry, commercial agriculture, or tourism. Central Zacatecas suffers from underutilized human capital owing to factors largely out of its control—failed federal agricultural programs; poor prices for its cattle, beans, and silver; and unfavorable political precedents.

Northern Coahuila has faced milder political and economic shocks: some revolutionary violence and recent fluctuations in the mining and metallurgical industries. Overall, however, the region is economically dynamic, with its power plants, maquiladoras, and commercial agriculture. U.S. migration is nevertheless high, because of the ease of crossing the border—due to simple proximity and to family ties across the border, which also help to explain the legalized status of many workers. Migration from Coahuila lacks the dimension of economic necessity that motivates migration from Zacatecas. It may be said that Coahuila has benefited from many political and economic forces which, although largely out of its control, have affected the state positively—for example, the increase in maquiladoras, growth of the (government-run) iron and steel industry in Monclova and Monterrey, trade liberalization, and agricultural research and extension through important universities in the region.

Patterns of U.S. Migration

The demographic, spatial, and temporal patterns of U.S. migration show similarities as well as differences between central Zacatecas and northern Coahuila. Both regions have high U.S. migration rates, which have risen markedly over the past several decades except for temporary lulls due to INS enforcement campaigns in the United States (in the 1950s) and industrial and agricultural development programs in Mexico (in the 1960s and 1970s). The average migrant is not too different from one of these regions to the other. He (nine-tenths are male) is young and well educated compared to his compatriots who choose not to migrate. In nine out of ten cases he is married, and he tends to have young children (all in the preteen category). This profile suggests the obligation young heads of household feel to support burgeoning families through the strategy of U.S. migration. It also suggests the risks and difficulties associated with the journey to the United States.

There are nevertheless important differences between the two regions. Central Zacatecas's migrants seek out California and, secondarily, Illinois for the superior pay they can earn there. The Zacatecas migrant stands apart from the nonmigrant more starkly than does the Coahuila migrant. In the smaller towns of more rural Zacatecas, some of the best-educated and most ambitious young men leave for the United States. This journey is a means of bypassing the restrictive economic and social pyramid that prevents them from getting good jobs in the urban areas of the region. Northern Coahuila's migrants, by comparison, take advantage of long-standing kinship ties with Texas. They have predominantly urban origins rather than rural ones, but do not face the barriers to economic and social mobility connected with tradition-bound central Mexico. For this reason they are not as strongly selected demographically. In contrast to central Zacatecas, U.S. migration from northern Coahuila not infrequently involves young men seeking adventure in *El Norte*. For them, U.S. migration is not as much a matter of economic necessity as it is to the Zacatecans.

Impacts on the Household Economy

The survey evidence supports a strong role for U.S. migrant remittances in Zacatecas. Active households (those that have sent a migrant to the United States in the past three years), as well as those with long-term U.S. migration experience (five years or more of cumulated work experience by all household members) have markedly higher levels of income and possessions than the households of inactive and short-term migrants. Furthermore, families of active and long-term migrants spend more on investment in agricultural inputs and on mixed consumption-investment purchases (including human capital expenditures such as medical care, education, and housing), and less on pure consumption than do inactive and short-term families. Migrant families spend more of their earnings outside of the hometown; but the great majority of the money spent remains within the local region. Finally, U.S. migration increases relative income inequalities among families but reduces the income differential between urban and rural areas.

In summary, then, rural families are able to use U.S. migration to better their economic and social situation and to improve their position vis-à-vis urban families. Migration for them is an alternative economic mobility ladder. In a broader sense, the process is replacing a narrow, traditional elite defined by control of the land, commerce, politics, and social life of the town with a broad-based migrant class whose influence is based upon U.S. earnings and the possessions and investments they make possible.

These findings tend to support the functionalist arguments and to support a generally positive view of U.S. migration. But to a degree, they also support structuralist arguments; little long-term regional development stems from migration; inequalities increase among families; and local social institutions suffer disintegration.

The impacts of U.S. migration on northern Coahuila are much less striking. Active and long-term U.S. migrant households have only slightly greater income and possessions than other households. In proportion to their income, migrant households consume more and invest less than other households—the reverse of the pattern seen in Zacatecas. There is only a slight tendency for migrant households to spend more outside the local community, and for income inequalities to increase between families and to diminish between rural and urban areas. Northern Coahuilan families find that U.S. migration is only one employment option among many.

Consumerism—improving one's lifestyle—is the goal for them, not economic survival. The region is similar in this regard to that across the border in Texas. Northern Coahuila is undoubtedly just as dependent on the United States as is central Zacatecas, but as a market for its products and a source for its purchases—not as a principal employer.

The Economic Base in Central Zacatecas

The discovery of U.S. migration's substantial impacts in central Zacatecas prompts a more detailed analysis of the effect of migrant remittances across the region relative to other external sources of income. Data for this analysis were obtained from both the household questionnaire and the establishment questionnaire. Complete economic and demographic data were ultimately obtained for 22 towns in the three municipios, ranging in size from 250 to 29,660 inhabitants.

The economic base analyses emphasize the importance of U.S. migration but also uncover another dynamic sector of growing importance—commercial agriculture. U.S. remittances, commercial agriculture, and private business each accounted for between one-third and one-fourth of the town's total income in 1987. However, of basic income (which is the lifeblood upon which other local sectors depend), U.S. remittances provided nearly half, compared to much lower proportions accounted for by private business, commercial agriculture, job commuting, government, and internal migrant remittances. Nevertheless, the estimation of income multipliers by regressing income against the three major basic sources (remittances, agriculture, and business) reveals that, per dollar earned, commercial agriculture has the greatest multiplier effect. This strong economic impact reflects the introduction, since the mid-1960s, of commercial peaches, grapes, broccoli, and other crops into the region. The towns fortunate enough to enjoy these investments have prospered greatly, while towns a few kilometers away (with essentially the same physical base) have languished. Often, as in the peach-producing towns in Jerez, U.S. remittances have provided seed money for commercial agriculture.

The multiplier analysis and several case studies suggest that commercial agricultural investment in central Zacatecas offers considerable promise for future development in the region. A number of towns are already prospering from such investment, alongside other towns without such investments. Since these other towns have basically the same physical bases, locations, and population sizes as those targeted for investment, we may conclude that they harbor undeveloped potential. The reason that this potential has not been realized lies in the insufficiency of entrepreneurship and of the political will to make the necessary investments.

The Impact of Trade Liberalization on Central Zacatecas

The issue of free trade is peripheral to the main purposes of this book, but it has now come to dominate Mexican-U.S. relations. The effects of trade liberalization in Mexico, which has been proceeding since at least 1984, have already been felt all over the country, including central Zacatecas and northern Coahuila. Thus, it is appropriate to conclude with a commentary on its actual and potential impacts, especially on emigrant municipios of central Mexico.

The topic of free trade and its effects on Mexico-U.S. migration is a controversial one. Some authors feel that it will reduce U.S. migration (Pazos 1990; Dornbusch 1990); others, that it will have little or no effect (Tamayo and Lozano 1991a; Cornelius 1991); and still others, that it will actually increase U.S. migration (Torres 1991; Barraclough 1991).

For Mexico in 1994—deeply involved in trade liberalization under the approved North American Free Trade Agreement—the fundamental question is still "which social groups . . . stand to gain [from free trade] . . . and which would probably lose and during what time period?" (Barraclough 1991, 2). The real question, then, concerns not the overall economic benefits but the distribution of benefits among different social groups and different regions. (There are also many important noneconomic questions of an environmental and cultural nature, which are not unrelated to the impacts discussed here.) Mexican intellectuals are to be found on both sides of the question. For example, the members of the so-called Cárdenas braintrust, including former finance minister Jesús Silva Herzog and writer Carlos Fuentes, argue that free trade based solely on low Mexican wages will benefit the wealthy but leave the majority of Mexican workers permanently impoverished (Orme 1991). On the other hand, political economist Luis Pazos (1990) and historian Enrique Krause (1991) both argue that free trade will bring economic and political reforms that will benefit all Mexicans, ultimately resulting in a more egalitarian, free-market democracy.

How is U.S.-Mexican trade liberalization affecting the migrant hearth region in general, and central Zacatecas in particular? Is it hurting subsistence corn-and-beans farmers, whose production is too inefficient to compete with unrestricted U.S. cereal and bean imports (Barkin 1990, 1991;

Barraclough 1991; Delgadillo 1992; Levy and van Wijnbergen 1991; López Arévalo and Villafuerte Solís 1991; Torres 1991)? The answer to this appears to be yes, to some degree: already, the internationalization of local agriculture has led to declines in corn production in central and southern Mexico (López Arévalo and Villafuerte Solís 1991). But the fact is that these farmers were already suffering from drought, poor marketing, and failed government programs long before trade liberalization. In central Zacatecas, it is true that some farmers are abandoning the production of corn and beans for more commercial products, chiefly horticultural ones.

Is trade liberalization bringing transnational export firms to central Zacatecas? The answer here appears to be yes. According to a SECOFI (Commerce and Industrial Development Secretariat) official, Zacatecas and Aguascalientes have been the two central Mexican states that have benefited most from recent trade liberalization (Valdez Marquez 1992). In Zacatecas, both SECOFI and SARH (Agriculture and Water Resources Secretariat) officials are assisting in efforts to bring in food processing plants that will subcontract local farmers to produce fruits and vegetables to be packaged locally and exported to the United States, as is done with broccoli in Luis Moya. In addition, maquiladoras producing furniture, automobile parts, children's clothing, and beer have been introduced into the state. Thus, despite the negative impacts that free trade has had on subsistence agriculture in the central region, commercial agriculture and manufacturing may continue to benefit from it.

The crux of the matter, however, is whether trade liberalization is inducing transnationals to locate in emigration-prone municipios of central Zacatecas such as Jerez and Villanueva. The answer here appears to be no. My analysis of data for 56 municipios in Zacatecas finds a negative correlation ($r_p = -0.284$) between U.S. migration and the incidence of major transnational investments around 1990. I also find a negative relationship ($r_p = -0.404$) between existing poverty and the incidence of major transnational investments (Jones 1992a), indicating that transnational corporations have sought out the already developed municipios in the industrial corridor from north of Zacatecas to north of Aguascalientes (fig. 7.1). I also find a positive relationship ($r_p = +0.422$) between U.S. migration and poverty, suggesting that such migration benefited the poorest municipios—a conclusion supported by other research in central Mexico (Jones 1992c; Levi 1990; Levi 1991). Since the transnationals in Zacatecas were all exporters, we may conclude that export expansion, at least in the short run, has been concentrated in the well-off, more centralized municipios in

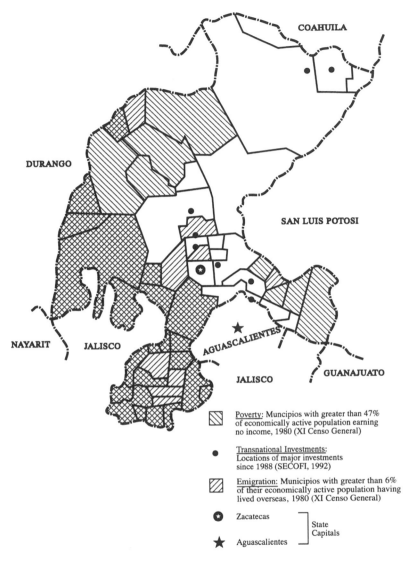

Figure 7.1 Poverty, investments, and emigration in Zacatecas

Zacatecas, not in the poorer, more peripheral, emigrant municipios of the state.

Other authors are pessimistic about the benefits of free trade to emigrant areas of central Mexico. Tamayo and Lozano do not acknowledge any benefits from transnational investments in Zacatecas (1991a, 1991b).

Cornelius (1991), in his restudy of three villages in the west-central region, finds minimal industrialization, almost no job commuting to nearby cities, and no reduction of U.S. emigration rates over time. He concludes that a "culture of out-migration" has developed in the region that is relatively immune to local development efforts, whether public or private. Díaz-Briquets and Weintraub (1991) espouse sustained economic development as the only viable alternative to migration, but conclude that "there is no simple way to significantly increase regional employment, and even if the number of jobs increases, a corresponding slowdown in undocumented migration may be some time in coming" (p. 13).

These evaluations may prove to be too pessimistic, but it yet too early to tell. There is clear evidence that in central Mexico the rate of U.S. migration is lower for municipios that are closer to regional growth centers (Jones 1988; Arroyo, de León, and Valenzuela 1991), implying that over the long term, such growth results in diffusion of income into (and the establishment of commuting from) the hinterlands of those centers. If such a trend is occurring, part of the explanation might be found in the notion of "product cycles," in which industrial production filters down the urban hierarchy as new industries mature (Park and Wheeler 1983; Cromley and Leinbach 1986). In Zacatecas, I have found a significant direct correlation between driving time to the closest growth center (defined as a city with a population above 100,000) and poverty level (defined as the percentage of the labor force who earned no income). Interestingly, this relationship weakened (both the correlation and the slope) between 1980 and 1990, implying the diffusion of growth into surrounding municipios, which—as table 6.2 suggests for the three central Zacatecas municipios—are sending significant numbers of commuters to jobs in nearby cities. I have also found, for Zacatecas, that population growth over the decade was inversely related to driving time from the closest growth center.

At any rate, the topic of free trade's impacts on rural central Mexico needs to be studied in much more detail. It cannot be assumed, as it is by some writers, that free trade will automatically lessen undocumented U.S. migration. If the participation in such trade spreads to the small farmer, then it might have that effect. However, it may be that rural, emigrant municipios are too geographically distant from new transnational investments to be affected by them at all. If that is the case, families living in these municipios will find themselves suffering from the negative effects of free trade—inflation in the prices of food and other goods along with declining domestic demand for the beans and corn they produce—while missing out on its principal positive impact—alternative employment. In the absence of policies that stimulate the diffusion of trade or that reinstate government assistance, U.S. migration from the poorer, peripheral municipios could continue and even increase.

Appendix A

Study Design

The west-central region of Mexico has been the focus for most of the Mexican village "impact" studies over the past 15 years (chapter 1). For the present study, it was decided to investigate U.S. migration impacts in two subregions that have been the focus of almost no impact studies—central Zacatecas and northern Coahuila (fig. 1.9). The selection of these subregions was based on their location in regions of relatively high undocumented migration to the United States (Jones 1988) and on prior field research in each of the regions (Jones and Murray 1986).

Within each of the subregions, particular municipios were selected according to several criteria. First, only municipios located within 80 miles (129 km) of a metropolitan municipio (one with a city of more than 50,000) were selected. This facilitated the investigation of the externalization of expenditures and of the role of commuting income relative to income from U.S. migration. Second, among these proximal municipios two types were chosen: (1) a smaller, agriculture-based municipio with no town larger than 10,000 population; and (2) a larger, urbanized municipio with a town of between 25,000 and 50,000 population. This variety enabled us to compare the impacts of migration at different urban scales.

Guided by these criteria, five municipios were selected (fig. 1.9). Three of them are in central Zacatecas, an area with one of the highest rates of U.S. emigration in Mexico (Jones 1988; Díez-Canedo 1984), and adjacent to the Los Altos de Jalisco area extensively studied in the literature. Two are in northern Coahuila, an area of high U.S. migration rates (Jones 1988), where few (if any) such studies have been carried out. In Zacatecas, both Villanueva and Luis Moya are rural, agricultural municipios, whereas Jerez is urban. Zacatecas is the adjacent metropolitan area. In Coahuila, Morelos is agriculture based, and San Juan de Sabinas (Nueva Rosita) is urban. Both Monclova and Piedras Negras are adjacent metropolitan areas.

Table A.1 Population and Sample in Subregions of Study

	Absolute Numbers			Proportions		
	Population		1987	Population		1987
	1980	1990	sample	1980	1990	sample
Central Zacatecas[a]						
< 5,000 people (rural)	64,217	56,256	388	.641	.537	.651
5,000+ people (urban)	35,933	48,593	208	.359	.463	.349
Total	100,150	104,849	596	1.000	1.000	1.000
Northern Coahuila[b]						
< 5,000 people (rural)	4,821	5,060	38	.112	.108	.082
5,000+ people (urban)	38,310	41,818	428	.888	.892	.918
Total	43,131	46,878	466	1.000	1.000	1.000

a. 3 municipios: Villanueva, Luis Moya, and Jerez
b. 2 municipios: Morelos and San Juan de Sabinas (Nueva Rosita)

Sampling Frame

Within these two subregions, towns and villages, stratified by size and by location within each municipio, were selected for interviewing, using an approximately random procedure (except that the *cabecera*, or municipio capital, was always interviewed). The number of interviewees by town was not in direct proportion to the town's census population, because such a procedure made the logistics of interviewing too difficult. However, in the sample, the relative number of urban and rural residents in the total population of each subregion was preserved. Considering that 2,500 was too small a number to reflect urban characteristics, I chose the figure of 5,000 persons in 1980 as the cutoff point for urban. In the eventual sample, the proportions of people by urban-rural classification were relatively close to those in the population in 1980 (table A.1). By 1990, the percentage urban for central Zacatecas had risen appreciably, due to the fact that the county seat of Luis Moya had grown to 5,366 in 1990, up from 4,045 in 1980, thereby crossing the urban threshold.

Individual households in each interview town were selected by a random procedure. A map of the town was obtained from the municipal president or *comisariado ejidal* (collective farm commissioner), or sketched out based on driving or walking through the town. The town was divided into sectors of approximately equal population, based on interviews with town officials. Homes were chosen randomly and in the same proportions within each of these sectors.

Survey Research Methodology

Three interview teams of two members each worked simultaneously in each town. One person interviewed, and the other recorded the information. The household interview schedule was four pages long, and included questions about the demographic characteristics of the household, economic condition of the household, migration history (Mexican and U.S.) of all family members, purchases and expenses of the household, support of community institutions, and opinions of the respondent on the advantages and disadvantages of U.S. migration on the town and on what the town needs to improve economically (appendix B). (In some of the towns, a two-page questionnaire was administered to a sample of public and private establishments; this is discussed in chapter 6.) The questionnaire was administered to the head of household or his/her spouse. The household questionnaire took between 15 and 30 minutes to complete.

The interviews in the state of Zacatecas were carried out between mid-January and late March of 1988; those in Coahuila were carried out between early April and early June 1988. A special extended study of Jerez municipio in Zacatecas was carried out in late June 1988.

As indicated in table A.1, 596 household questionnaires were completed in central Zacatecas, 65 percent of them in rural areas; whereas in northeastern Coahuila 466 questionnaires were completed, only 8 percent of which were in rural areas. The rural-urban dimension indexes many other demographic aspects of life in Mexico.

Household Questionnaire

Municipio _____

Localidad _____

Entrevistador(es) _____

Fecha _____

ENCUESTA CASERA

La Base Económica del México Rural

Entrevistador: La encuesta debe incluir los ingresos y gastos de todos los miembros de la casa. "Casa" significa los miembros de una familia viviendo juntos, con sus propias habitaciones y su propio presupuesto.

Pida: ¿Quién tendrá el mejor conocimiento de los ingresos y gastos de la casa? (Si presente) ¿Podríamos entrevistar a él/ella/ellos?

A. *Datos Demográficos de la Casa*

1. Relación del respondiente al jefe de la casa (JC) _____
2a. JC: estado civil y año de casarse _____
b. Sexo del JC _____
3. Lugar de nacimiento del JC (loc., estado) _____
4a. Residencia previa del JC (loc., estado) _____
b. ¿Cuándo vivió allá últimamente? (año) _____
5. Número de años cursados del JC _____
6. Favor de dar los edades de todos los miembros de la familia:
JC _____
Esposa(o) _____
Hijos(as) [e.g., M12, F14, etc; circunde los que no viven aquí]

_____

Otros [especifique relación/edad] _____

7. Favor de indicar las ocupaciones locales de los miembros de la casa:
    miembro   1. _____   2. _____
    rel. al JC   *ocup. local*   *tipo de empresa*   *localidad de ocup.*

    _____ _____ _____ _____

    _____ _____ _____ _____

B. *Condición Económica de la Casa*

8. Posesiones de la casa (marque todos aplicables):
    luz _____ drenaje (en la casa)_____ teléfono_____ refrigerador_____
    lavadora _____ máquina de coser_____ televisión _____ estéreo_____
    carro_____ camioneta _____

9. Características de la casa:
    a. Materiales de construcción: techo   _____
                                    piso   _____
    b. Número de cuartos en la casa (inclu. cocina)   _____
    c. ¿Es usted dueño de su casa?   sí ___ no___

10. Tierra cultivable de la casa:
    a. ¿Cuántas hectáreas de tierra cultivable tiene la casa?   _____
    b. ¿Cuántas hectáreas son de riego?   _____
    c. ¿En su tierra, se utiliza insecticida química?   sí ___ no___
    d. . . . semillas mejoradas?   sí ___ no___
    e. ¿Se cultiva su tierra por Ud. o por miembros de su casa? sí ___ no___
    f. ¿Cultiva Ud. tierra a medias?   sí ___ no___

11a. ¿Tiene su familia un negocio?   sí ___ no___
    b. Tipo de negocio   _____
    c. ¿Se maneja su negocio por Ud. o miembros de la casa? sí ___ no___

C. *Historia de la Migración*

12a. ¿Ha trabajado cualquier miembro de esta casa *en otra
    parte de México* (i.e., como migrante, fuera reg. local)? sí ___ no___
    b. ¿ . . . en los últimos 3 años (1985–87)?   sí ___ no___
    Favor de listar localidades y tipos de trabajo (últimos 3 años):
    miembro   1. _____   2. _____
    rel. al JC   *localidad*   *tipo de trabajo*

    _____ _____ _____ _____

    _____ _____ _____ _____

13a. ¿Ha trabajado un miembro de esta casa *en los EUA?*   sí ___ no___

   b. ¿En cualquier tiempo, ha recibido esta casa dinero de
      familiares trabajando en los EUA?   sí ___ no___

   c. ¿Ha recibido dinero de los EUA en 1987?   sí ___ no___

14. Favor de decirnos acerca de todos *los viajes a los EUA,*
    para trabajar, que emprendieron los miembros de esta familia.

	Miembro de la familia		
	1	2	3
a. Relación al JC (y edad)	___	___	___
b. ¿Está en EUA ahora?	___	___	___
c. No. de viajes totales	___	___	___
d. Años de los viajes (listar—e.g.	___	___	___
67, 72, 85, 87, utilizando 2 líneas)	___	___	___
e. Destino principal del primer viaje			
(ciudad)	___	___	___
(estado)	___	___	___
f. # de años, meses, primer viaje	___	___	___
g. Tipo de trabajo, primer viaje	___	___	___
h. Tipo de papeles, primer viaje	___	___	___
i. # de familiares ya en los EUA, p.v.	___	___	___
j. Destino principal del último viaje			
(ciudad)	___	___	___
(estado)	___	___	___
k. # de años, meses, último viaje	___	___	___
l. Tipo de trabajo, último viaje	___	___	___
m. Tipo de papeles, último viaje	___	___	___
n. # de familiares ya en los EUA, u.v.	___	___	___
o. Tiempo total en los EUA, del pri-	___	___	___
mer al último viaje (años, meses)			

15. Ahora, favor de decirnos acerca los miembros de la familia actual-
    mente viviendo en los EUA (no JC; con 2 años o más sin regresar,
    o casado con su familia viviendo en EUA):

	Miembro de la familia		
	1	2	3
a. Relación al JC (y edad)	___	___	___
b. Años de los viajes (listar)	___	___	___
	___	___	___

c. Destino principal, último viaje (cd.) ———— ———— ————
(estado) ———— ———— ————
d. # de años, meses, último viaje ———— ———— ————
e. Tipo de trabajo, último viaje ———— ———— ————
f. Tipo de papeles, último viaje ———— ———— ————
g. Tiempo total en los EUA, años, ———— ———— ————
meses

D. *Compras y Gastos de la Casa*

16. ¿Cuáles fueron sus mayores categorías de compras y gastos en 1987, indicando la cantidad (en pesos o dólares) de cada compra o gasto, su localidad principal, y el fuente principal de fondos por la compra? INCLUYA COMPRAS DE ARTICULOS TRAIDOS DE LOS EUA EN 1987.
[Nota al entrevistador: En caso de un negocio familiar, comprende solamente las compras/gastos que pertenecen a la familia]. NOTA: *Fuentes de fondos:* Loc= trabajo local, US= trab. en US, MX= trab. en otra región, Pres= préstamo en 1987, Ahor= Ahorro del año anterior.]

Tipo de compra/gasto	*Pesos*	*Localidad principal*	*Fuente*
Comprar tierra cultivable	————	————	————
Arrendar tierra	————	————	————
Comprar ganado	————	————	————
Comprar camión	————	————	————
Comprar maquinaria	————	————	————
Comprar insectic., ferts., semillas	————	————	————
Comida	————	————	————
Ropa	————	————	————
Comprar casa	————	————	————
Construir o mejorar la casa	————	————	————
Alquilar casa	————	————	————
Aparatos domésticos, muebles	————	————	————
Comprar carro	————	————	————
Gastos medicales	————	————	————
Gastos educacionales	————	————	————
Intereses (préstamo =———— $\times$ r)	————	————	————

Otros (e.g., recreación, utilidades,
impuestos, gastos vehiculares, etc.):

(Especifique: _____ _____ _____ _____

_____ _____ _____ _____)

17. ¿Aproximadamente cuánto dinero *ahorró* su familia
en 1987 (de su ingresos en 1987)?   _____ pesos

18. ¿Cuánto, aproximadamente, recibió su casa de
familiares trabajando en los EUA en 1987?   _____ dólares

19. ¿Cuánto recibió su casa de familiares trabajando en
otras partes de la república mexicana, en 1987?   _____ pesos

E. *Apoyo a las Instituciones de la Comunidad*

20. Nos gustaría saber si, en 1987, su casa contribuyó con
alguna cantidad a cada de los siguientes:

pesos

a. Su familia grande   _____

b. Su iglesia local (pida: ¿es católico? si no, cuál) _____ _____

c. Proyectos colectivos de la comunidad
(escuela, obras públicas, fiestas, etc.
Especifique cuáles _____)   _____

F. *Opiniones del Respondiente*

21. [Solamente a las casas con experiencia migratoria
en los EUA desde 1980 y adelante]

a. ¿Ha demorado o impedido su volver a los EUA
o su regresar a México (Ud. y otros miembros de la familia)
el ley nuevo de Simpson/Rodino?   sí ___ no___

b. ¿Han tenido problemas en encontrar trabajo,
miembros de su familia, debido al nuevo ley?   sí ___ no___
¿Quiénes?_____

22. ¿Qué opina {Ud.} de las ventajas y desventajas de la migración a los
EUA, a este pueblo/ciudad (incluyendo social, familial, económico,
etc.)?

23. ¿Qué opina Ud. que se hace falta para mejorar la economía local?

Establishment Questionnaire

Municipio _____

Localidad _____

Entrevistador(es) _____

Fecha _____

Tipo de establecimiento _____

ENCUESTA ESTABLECIMIENTO

La Base Económica del México Rural

Entrevistador: Esta encuesta es por administrarse al dueño/gerente del establecimiento; al administrador público; o al director de la organización privada.

A. *Pérfil del Establecimiento*

1. ¿Cuáles productos o servicios ofrece? (listar)_____

2a. ¿Cuándo se estableció esta unidad, en esta localidad? (año) _____

b. ¿Desde cuándo es Ud. dueño/gerente del estab.? (mes, año)_____

c. (Si este estab. es una división o sucursal de una companía más grande) ¿Dónde se encuentra la oficina matriz? _____

3. ¿Cuántos empleados tiene, incluyendo Ud. mismo?

a. Tiempo completo   _____

b. Tiempo incompleto   _____

B. *Ventas o Presupuesto Operacional de este Establecimiento*
    [Nota: Si el establecimiento es un negocio, pida ventas; si es una oficina del gobierno, o una organización sin fin lucrativo, pida presupuesto operacional.]

4. Aproximadamente cuál porcentaje de sus ventas/presupuesto del año pasado (1987) derivó de los clientes/fuentes localizados:
   a. Dentro de esta localidad _____%
   b. Afuera de esta localidad _____%
   c. Afuera de la región local (_____) _____%
   d. Otras partes de la región local _____%

5a. ¿Vende este establecimiento productos o servicios a otros establecimientos? sí ___ no___

   b. Favor de permitarnos a preguntar sobre algunos de sus clientes mayores, incluyendo su nombre, tipo, y localización (1987) [Nota: un "cliente mayor" significa 25% o más de su ingreso]:

   Nombre, tipo de establecimiento   *Localización (ciudad, estado)*
   _____   _____
   _____   _____

6. Por favor, indique aproximadamente sus ventas totales/presupuesto operacional en el año pasado: _____ pesos

C. *Historia Migratoria del Dueño/Gerente/Administrador*

7a. ¿Ha trabajado Ud. en otra parte de México? sí ___ no___
   b. ¿. . . . en los últimos 3 años (1985–87)? sí ___ no___
   c. (Si el estab. es un negocio) ¿Utilizó los ingresos de este trabajo para financiar la operación o la compra de este negocio? sí ___ no___
   d. ¿Ha trabajado Ud. en los EUA? sí ___ no___
   e. Número total de viajes a los EUA para trabajar _____
   f. Años de los viajes (e.g., 76, 85, 86 . . .) (listar) _____
   g. Tiempo total en EUA (años, meses) _____
   h. ¿Qué tipo de papeles llevó en su último viaje? _____
   i. (Si el estab. es un negocio) ¿Utilizó los ingresos de este trabajo para financiar la operación o la compra de este negocio? sí ___ no___

D. *Gastos y Factores de la Producción*

8. *En 1987,* aproximadamente cuál fue sus gastos totales por:

   Pesos (o %):
   a. Salarios y beneficios pagado a sus empleados _____
   b. Inventorio (provisiones, materias primas, sub-productos, productos a mayor, etc.— cuales componen su producto) _____

Pesos

c. Servicios (luz, agua, teléfono, seguros, etc.)   ———————

d. Renta (edificio, tierra)   ———————

e. Otros (especifique: ————————————————) ———————

f. ¿Aproximadamente cuál fue su margen de ganancia
    en 1987?   ———————%

9. Favor de indicar aproximadamente el número de sus empleados, in-
    cluyendo usted, residiendo en diferentes localidades:

    Localidad   *Núm. de empleados*

    ————————————————   ————————————————

    ————————————————   ————————————————

    ————————————————   ————————————————

    ————————————————   ————————————————

10. Favor de indicar las localidades donde los gastos siguientes se hi-
    cieron *en 1987*:

    Loc. único o principal   *Otros localidades*

    a. Inventorio   ————————————————   ————————————————

    b. Servicios   ————————————————   ————————————————

    c. Renta   ————————————————   ————————————————

    d. Otros (esp.)

    ————————————   ————————————————   ————————————————

    ————————————   ————————————————   ————————————————

E. *Opiniones del Dueño/Gerente/Administrador*

11. ¿Qué opina usted que se hace falta para mejorar la economía local?

References

Adelman, Irma, J. Edward Taylor, and Stephen Vogel
1988 "Life in a Mexican Village: A SAM Perspective." *Journal of Development Studies* 25 (October): 5–24.
Arroyo Alejandre, Jesús, Adrian de León Arias, and Basilia Valenzuela Varela
1991 "Patterns of Migration and Regional Development in the State of Jalisco, Mexico." In Sergio Díaz-Briquets and Sidney Weintraub, eds., *Regional and Sectoral Development in Mexico as Alternatives to Migration*. Boulder: Westview, pp. 47–87.
Barkin, David
1990 *Distorted Development: Mexico in the World Economy*. Boulder: Westview.
1991 "About Face." *NACLA Report on the Americas* 24, no. 6 (May): 30–38.
Barraclough, Solon L.
1991 "Some Questions About the Implications for Rural Mexicans of the Proposed North American Free Trade Agreement (NAFTA)." Paper presented at the XI Seminario de Economía Agrícola, November 22, 1991, UNAM, Instituto de Economía.
Benke, David Allen
1982 Opportunity Structures Facing Indocumentados in Two Texas Metropolitan Areas: A Case Study of San Antonio and Austin. M.A. thesis, University of Texas at Austin.
Bohning, W. R.
1975 "Some Thoughts on Emigration from the Mediterranean Basin." *International Labor Review* 111, no. 3: 251–77.
Brana-Shute, R., and G. Brana-Shute
1982 "The Magnitude and Impact of Remittances in the Eastern Caribbean: A Research Note." In William F. Stinner, Klaus Albuquerque, and Roy S. Bryce-Laporte, eds., *Return Migration and Remittances: Developing a Caribbean Perspective*. Washington, D.C.: Smithsonian Institution, pp. 267–89.
Brown, Lawrence A.
1981 *Innovation Diffusion: A New Perspective*. New York: Methuen.
Cardoso, Lawrence A.
1980 *Mexican Immigration to the United States, 1897–1931*. Tucson: University of Arizona Press.

Cobbe, James
1982   "Emigration and Development in Southern Africa, with Special Refer-
        ence to Lesotho." *International Migration Review* 16, no. 4: 837–68.
Conway, Dennis
1985   "Remittance Impacts on Development in the Eastern Caribbean." *Bul-
        letin of Eastern Caribbean Affairs* 11, nos. 4 and 5 (Sept.–Dec.): 31–40.
Cornelius, Wayne A.
1976   *Mexican Migration to the United States: The View from Rural Sending
        Communities.* Cambridge: Massachusetts Institute of Technology, Cen-
        ter for International Studies.
1978   *Mexican Migration to the United States: Causes, Consequences, and U.S.
        Responses.* Cambridge: Massachusetts Institute of Technology, Center for
        International Studies.
1990   *Labor Migration to the United States: Development Outcomes and Alter-
        natives in Mexican Sending Communities.* Final Report to the Commis-
        sion for the Study of International Migration and Cooperative Economic
        Development. La Jolla: Center for U.S.–Mexican Studies, University of
        California at San Diego.
1991   "Labor Migration to the U.S.: Development Outcomes and Alternatives
        in Mexican Sending Communities." In Sergio Díaz-Briquets and Sidney
        Weintraub, eds., *Regional and Sectoral Development in Mexico as Alter-
        natives to Migration.* Boulder: Westview, pp. 89–131.
Corwin, Arthur F., ed.
1978   *Immigrants—and Immigrants: Perspectives on Mexican Labor Migration
        to the United States.* Westport, Conn.: Greenwood Press.
Cromley, Robert G., and Thomas R. Leinbach
1986   "External Control of Nonmetropolitan Industry in Kentucky." *Profes-
        sional Geographer* 38, no. 4: 332–42.
Cross, Harry E., and James A. Sandos
1981   *Across the Border: Rural Development in Mexico and Recent Migration to
        the United States.* Berkeley: Institute of Governmental Studies, University
        of California.
Delgadillo, Javier
1992   "El Sector Agropecuario en Transición: Los Retos de Modernización."
        Paper presented at the 13th National Congress of Geography, Aguasca-
        lientes, May 27–29.
de Oliver, Miguel
1993   "The Hegemonic Cycle and Free Trade: The U.S. and Mexico." Paper
        presented at the 89th Annual Meeting, Association of American Geog-
        raphers, Atlanta, April.
Development Data Book, 2d ed.
1988   Washington, D.C.: World Bank.
de Walt, Billie R.
1979   *Modernization in a Mexican Village.* Cambridge: Cambridge University
        Press.

Díaz-Briquets, Sergio, and Sidney Weintraub, eds.
 1991   *Regional and Sectoral Development in Mexico as Alternatives to Migration.* Boulder: Westview, pp. 3–13.

Diccionario Porrva: Historia, Biografía, y Geografía de México
 1964   Mexico, D.F.

Díez-Canedo, Juan
 1984   *La Migración Indocumentada de México a los Estados Unidos: Un Nuevo Enfoque.* Mexico, D.F.: Fondo de Cultura Económica.

Dinerman, Ina R.
 1982   *Migrants and Stay-at-Homes: A Comparative Study of Rural Migration from Michoacán, Mexico.* La Jolla: Center for U.S.–Mexican Studies, University of California at San Diego, Monograph Series no. 5.

Dornbusch, Rudiger
 1990   "Issues Related to a Free Trade Agreement with Mexico." *Texas Perspective* 3: 30–39.

Dos Santos, T.
 1973   "The Crisis of Development and the Problem of Dependence in Latin America." In H. Bernstein, ed., *Underdevelopment and Development: The Third World Today.* Harmondsworth, Eng.: Penguin Books, pp. 57–81.

Eikaas, Faith E.
 1979   "You Can't Go Home Again? Culture Shock and Patterns of Adaptation, Norwegian Refugees." In Carolyn Garrett Pool, ed., *Papers in Anthropology* 20, no. 1 (Spring): 105–15.

Enciclopedia de México, 2d ed., vol. 3.
 1977   Mexico, D.F.: Editorio Mexicana, S.A. de C.V.

Espenshade, Edward B., Jr., ed.
 1990   *Goode's World Atlas*, 18th ed. Chicago: Rand McNally.

Fehrenbach, T. R.
 1973   *Fire and Blood: A History of Mexico.* New York: Macmillan.

Fergany, Nader
 1982   "The Impact of Emigration on National Development in the Arab Region: The Case of the Yemen Arab Republic." *International Migration Review* 16: 757–80.

Foster, George M.
 1967   *Tzintzuntzan: Mexican Peasants in a Changing World.* Boston: Little, Brown.

Frank, Andre G.
 1981   *Crisis: In the Third World.* New York: Holmes and Meier.

Friedmann, John
 1966   *Regional Development Policy: A Case Study of Venezuela.* Cambridge: MIT Press.

Fromm, Eric, and Michael Maccoby
 1970   *Social Character in a Mexican Village: A Socio-Psychoanalytic Study.* Englewood Cliffs, N.J.: Prentice Hall.

Gamio, Manuel
   1930   *Mexican Immigration to the United States: A Study of Human Migration and Adjustment.* Chicago: University of Chicago Press.
Garrison, Charles B.
   1972   "The Impact of New Industry: An Application of the Economic Base Multiplier to Small Rural Areas." *Land Economics* 48: 329–37.
Gonzalez-Casanova, P.
   1965   "Internal Colonialism and National Development." *Studies in International Comparative Development* 1, no. 4: 27–37.
Griffiths, Stephen L.
   1979   "Emigration and Entrepreneurship in a Philippine Peasant Village." In Carolyn Garrett Pool, ed., *Papers in Anthropology* 20, no. 1 (Spring): 127–43.
Grindle, Merilee S.
   1988   *Searching for Rural Development: Labor Migration and Employment in Mexico.* Ithaca, N.Y.: Cornell University Press.
Hancock, Richard H.
   1959   *The Role of the Bracero in the Economic and Cultural Dynamics of Mexico: A Case Study of Chihuahua.* Stanford, Calif.: Hispanic American Society.
Hirschman, Albert O.
   1958   *The Strategy of Economic Development.* New Haven: Yale University Press.
Hoskin, Marilyn, and Roy C. Fitzgerald
   1989   "German Immigration Policy and Politics." In Michael C. LeMay, ed., *The Gatekeepers: Comparative Immigration Policy.* New York: Praeger, pp. 95–118.
INEGI (Instituto Nacional de Estadística Geográfica e Informática)
   1980   *X Censo General de Población y Vivienda.* México, D.F. *Integración Territorial, Estado de Zacatecas.*
   1990   *XI Censo General de Población y Vivienda.* México, D.F., state volumes for Zacatecas and Coahuila, and Resumen General.
James, Stuart, and Michael Kearney
   1981   *Causes and Effects of Agricultural Labor Migration from the Mixteca of Oaxaca to California.* La Jolla: Center for U.S.–Mexican Studies, University of California at San Diego, working paper no. 28.
Johnson, Alan G.
   1988   *Statistics.* San Diego: Harcourt Brace Jovanovich.
Jones, Richard C.
   1984   "Macro-Patterns of Undocumented Migration between Mexico and the U.S." in Richard C. Jones, ed., *Patterns of Undocumented Migration: Mexico and the United States.* Totowa, N.J.: Rowman and Allanheld, pp. 33–57.
   1986   "Explaining Origin Patterns of Mexican Undocumented Migration." Final Report, National Geographic Society Grant no. 2959-84.
   1987   "An Economic Base Analysis of Poteet, Texas." Report submitted to the

City Administrator (July). Authored with the assistance of Charles Bunnell, Dianne Caddel, and Deborah Stutz.

1988   "Micro-Source Regions of Mexican Undocumented Migration." *National Geographic Research* 4, no. 1: 11–22.

1991   "The Urban Economic Base in a Trans-Border Setting: A Case Study of Two Towns." *Journal of Borderlands Studies* 6, no. 1: 69–90.

1992a   "U.S. Migration: An Alternative Economic Mobility Ladder for Rural Central Mexico." *Social Science Quarterly* 73, no. 3: 496–510.

1992b   "The Impact of Trade Liberalization on the Rural North-Central Region of Mexico" Paper presented at the 13th National Congress of Geography, Aguascalientes, May 27–29.

1992c   "Remittances and Inequality in Rural Central Mexico: A Question of Scale." Paper presented at the annual meeting of the Association of American Geographers, San Diego, April 18–22.

1994   "Mexican Undocumented Migration Before and After Immigration Reform." Manuscript.

————, ed.

1990   "Comprehensive Urban Study of Castroville (Texas)." Report submitted to the City of Castroville and the UTSA Center for Economic Development (July).

Jones, Richard C., and David Alvírez

1994   "Migration, Trade Liberalization, and Socioeconomic Change in the Altiplano of San Luis Potosí." Manuscript.

Jones, Richard C., Richard J. Harris, and Avelardo Valdez

1984   "Occupational and Spatial Mobility of Migrants from Dolores Hidalgo, Guanajuato." In Richard C. Jones, ed., *Patterns of Undocumented Migration: Mexico and the United States.* Totowa, N.J.: Rowman and Allanheld, pp. 159–82.

Jones, Richard C., and Maria M. Maya

1991   "International Migration and Reinvestment: Evidence from Central Mexico" Paper presented at the national meeting of the Association of American Geographers, Miami, Fla., Apr. 16.

Jones, Richard C., and William Breen Murray

1986   "Occupational and Spatial Mobility of Temporary Mexican Migrants to the U.S.: A Comparative Analysis." *International Migration Review* 20, no. 4: 973–85.

Jordan, Terry G., John Bean, Jr., and William M. Holmes

1984   *Texas: A Geography.* Boulder: Westview.

Keely, Charles B., and Bao Nga Tran

1989   "Remittances from Labor Migration: Evaluations, Performance, and Implications." *International Migration Review* 23 (Fall 1989): 500–25.

Kirwan, F. X.

1981   "The Impact of Labor Migration on the Jordanian Economy." *International Migration Review* 15, no. 4: 671–95.

154   References

Krause, Enrique
1991   "The Historic Dimensions of Free Trade with Mexico." *Wall Street Journal*, May 24, p. A11.
Kritz, Mary M., Charles B. Keely, and Silvano M. Tomasi, eds.
1981   *Global Trends in Migration: Theory and Research on Population Movements.* Staten Island, N.Y.: Center for Migration Studies.
Layton-Henry, Zig
1989   "British Immigration Policy and Politics." In Michael C. LeMay, ed., *The Gatekeepers: Comparative Immigration Policy.* New York: Praeger, pp. 59–93.
Levi, Silvana
1990   "Factores de Cambio en México Rural." *Actas del VI Coloquio de Geografía Rural.*
1991   "Rural Change and Circular Migration to the United States: A Case Study from Michoacán, Mexico." *Investigaciones Geográficas* no. 23: 377–94.
Levy, Santiago, and Sweder van Wijnbergen
1991   "Labor Markets, Migration, and Welfare: Agriculture in the Mexico–U.S. Free Trade Agreement." Draft report, World Bank, June.
Lewis, Oscar
1963   *Life in a Mexican Village: Tepoztlan Restudied.* Urbana: University of Illinois Press.
Ling, L. Huan-Ming
1984   "East Asian Migration to the Middle East: Causes, Consequences, and Considerations." *International Migration Review* 18 (Spring): 19–36.
López Arévalo, Jorge, and Daniel Villafuerte Solís
1991   "La Producción de Maíz en Chiapas ante el Tratado de Libre Comercio." Paper presented at the XI Seminario de Economía Agricola, November 22, UNAM, Instituto de Economía.
López Castro, Gustavo
1986   *La Casa Dividida: Un Estudio de Caso Sobre la Migración a Estados Unidos en un Pueblo Michoacano.* Zamora: Colegio de Michoacán.
Lozano, Fernando A., Alicia Cuevas, Bertha Largue, and B. Nieto
1985   *La Expulsión de Trabajadores Rurales a los Estados Unidos: El Caso de Jerez, Zacatecas.* México, D.F.: Ministerio de Planificación y Presupuesto, Departamento de Análisis de Mercados de Trabajo.
Massey, Douglas S.
1986   "The Settlement Process Among Mexican Migrants to the United States." *American Sociological Review* 51 (October): 670–84.
Massey, Douglas S., Rafael Alarcon, Jorge Durand, and Humberto Gonzalez
1987   *Return to Aztlán: The Social Process of International Migration from Western Mexico.* Berkeley: University of California Press.
McArthur, Harold J., Jr.
1979   "The Effects of Overseas Work on Return Migrants and Their Home

Communities: A Philippine Case." In Carolyn Garrett Pool, ed., *Papers in Anthropology* 20, no. 1 (Spring): 85–104.

McCray, John P.
1989   *Maquila Sourcing Opportunities for San Antonio Businesses.* San Antonio: Department of Economic and Employment Development.

Mendonsa, Eugene
1982   "Benefits of Migration as a Personal Strategy in Nazare, Portugal." *International Migration Review* 16, no. 3: 635–45.

Mines, Richard
1981   *Developing a Community Tradition of Migration: A Field Study in Rural Zacatecas, Mexico, and California Settlement Areas.* La Jolla: Program in U.S.–Mexican Studies, University of California, San Diego, monograph no. 3.

Morrill, Richard, Gary L. Gaile, and Grant I. Thrall
1988   *Spatial Diffusion.* Scientific Geography Series, vol. 10. Newbury Park, Calif.: Sage Publications.

Morrison, P., and L. Sinkin
1982   "International Migration in the Dominican Republic: Implications for Development Planning." *International Migration Review* 16: 819–36.

Naisbitt, John
1984   *Megatrends: Ten New Directions Transforming Our Lives.* New York: Warner Books.

Newcomb, W. W., Jr.
1961   *The Indians of Texas: From Prehistoric to Modern Times.* Austin: University of Texas Press.

North, David S., and Marion F. Houstoun
1976   *The Characteristics and Role of Illegal Aliens in the U.S. Labor Market: An Exploratory Study.* Washington, D.C.: Linton, for the Employment and Training Administration, U.S. Department of Labor.

Orme, William A., Jr.
1991   "The Sunbelt Moves South." *NACLA Report on the Americas* 24, no. 6 (May): 10–21.

Park, Sam Ock, and James O. Wheeler
1983   "The Filtering Down Process in Georgia: The Third Stage in the Product Life Cycle." *Professional Geographer* 35, no. 1: 18–31.

Pazos, Luis
1990   *Free Trade: Mexico–U.S.A.: Myths and Facts.* México, D.F.: Editorial Diana.

Piore, Michael J.
1979   *Birds of Passage: Migrant Labor and Industrial Societies.* Cambridge: Cambridge University Press.

Pi-Sunyer, Oriol
1973   *Zamora: Change and Continuity in a Mexican Town.* New York: Holt, Rinehart, and Winston.

Portes, Alejandro
    1978   "Migration and Underdevelopment." *Politics and Society* 8: 1–48.
Ranney, Susan, and Sherrie Kossoudji
    1983   "Profiles of Temporary Mexican Labor Migrants to the United States."
            Population and Development Review 9, no. 3: 475–93.
Reichert, Joshua S.
    1981   "The Migrant Syndrome: Seasonal U.S. Labor Migration and Rural De-
            velopment in Central Mexico." *Human Organization* 40, no. 1: 56–66.
Reichert, Joshua S., and Douglas S. Massey
    1979   "Patterns of U.S. Migration from a Mexican Sending Community: A
            Comparison of Legal and Illegal Migrants." *International Migration
            Review* 13, no. 4: 599–623.
Reitsma, H. A., and J. M. G. Kleinpenning
    1985   *The Third World in Perspective.* Totowa, N.J.: Rowman and Allanheld.
Rhoades, Robert E.
    1979   "From Caves to Main Street: Return Migration and the Transformation
            of a Spanish Village." In Carolyn Garrett Pool, ed., *Papers in Anthropol-
            ogy* 20, no. 1 (Spring): 57–74.
Richardson, Bonham
    1983   *Caribbean Migrants: Environment and Human Survival on St. Kitts and
            Nevis.* Knoxville: University of Tennessee Press.
Roberts, Kenneth D.
    1982   "Agrarian Structure and Labor Mobility in Rural Mexico." *Population
            and Development Review* 8: 299–322.
Robinson, J. G.
    1980   "Estimating the Approximate Size of the Illegal Alien Population in the
            United States." Paper presented at the Census Advisory Committee
            Meeting, American Statistical Association Meetings, Washington, D.C.
Rogers, Everett M.
    1983   *Diffusion of Innovations.* New York: Free Press.
Rostow, W. W.
    1960   *The Stages of Economic Growth.* Cambridge: Cambridge University Press.
Rubenstein, Hymie
    1982   "The Impact of Remittances in the Rural English-Speaking Caribbean."
            In William F. Stinner, Klaus Albuquerque, and Roy S. Bryce-Laporte,
            eds., *Return Migration and Remittances: Developing a Caribbean Per-
            spective.* Washington, D.C.: Smithsonian Institution, pp. 237–65.
Russell, Sharon S.
    1986   "Remittances from International Migration: A Review in Perspective."
            World Development 14, no. 6: 677–96.
Salt, John
    1989   "A Comparative Overview of International Trends and Types." *Interna-
            tional Migration Review* 23 (Fall): 431–56.
Samora, Julian
    1971   *Los Mojados: The Wetback Story.* Notre Dame: University of Notre Dame
            Press.

Secretaria de Agricultura y Recursos Hidráulicos, México
1982   *Diagnóstico Agroindustrial: Zacatecas.* Coordinación General de Desarrollo Agroindustrial, México, D.F.
Secretaria de Educación Pública, México
1982   *Zacatecas: Suelo Metálico Bajo las Nopaleras.* State [Zacatecas] monograph, working paper.
Shadow, Robert D.
1979   "Differential Out-Migration: A Comparison of Internal and International Migration from Villa Guerrero, Jalisco (Mexico)." In Fernando Camara and Robert Van Kemper, eds., *Migration Across Frontiers: Mexico and the United States.* Albany: Institute for Mesoamerican Studies, State University of New York, pp. 67–83.
Shah, Nasra M.
1983   "Pakistani Workers in the Middle East: Volume, Trends, and Consequences." *International Migration Review* 17, no. 3: 410–24.
Shrestha, Nanda R.
1985   "The Political Economy of Economic Underdevelopment and External Migration in Nepal." *Political Geography Quarterly* 4 (October): 289–306.
Simcox, David E.
1988   "Illegal Immigration: Counting the Shadow Population." In David E. Simcox, ed., *U.S. Immigration in the 1980s.* Boulder: Westview, pp. 23–34.
Simpson, Eyler N.
1937   *The Ejido: Mexico's Way Out.* Chapel Hill: University of North Carolina Press.
Síntesis Geográfica de Zacatecas
1981   México, D.F.: Secretaria de Programación y Presupuesto, INEGI.
Stark, Oded, J. Edward Taylor, and Schlomo Yitzhaki
1986   "Remittances and Inequality." *Economic Journal* 96 (Sept.): 722–40.
Swanson, Jon C.
1979   "The Consequences of Emigration for Economic Development: A Review of the Literature." In Carolyn Garrett Pool, ed., *Papers in Anthropology* 20, no. 1 (Spring): 39–56.
Tamayo, Jesús, and Fernando Lozano
1991a   "The Economic and Social Development of High Emigration Areas in the State of Zacatecas: Antecedents and Policy Alternatives." In Sergio Díaz-Briquets and Sidney Weintraub, eds., *Regional and Sectoral Development in Mexico as Alternatives to Migration.* Boulder: Westview, pp. 15–46.
1991b   "Mexican Perceptions on Rural Development and Migration of Workers to the United States and Actions Taken, 1970–1988." In Sergio Díaz-Briquets and Sidney Weintraub, eds., *Regional and Sectoral Development in Mexico as Alternatives to Migration.* Boulder: Westview, pp. 363–87.
Taylor, Edward J.
1987   "Undocumented Mexico–U.S. Migration and the Returns to House-

holds in Rural Mexico." *American Journal of Agricultural Economics* 69 (August): 626–38.

Taylor, Paul S.
1930   *Mexican Labor in the United States.* New York: Arno Press, repr. 1970.

Tiebout, Charles M.
1962   *The Community Economic Base Study.* New York: Committee for Economic Development.

Torres Torres, Felipe
1991   "No a la Eutanacia del Maíz en México." Paper presented at XI Seminario de Economía Agrícola, November 22, 1991, UNAM, Instituto de Economía.

Valdez Marquez, Francisco
1992   Sub-director de Promoción, SECOFI, Zacatecas. Personal interview, March 16.

Villarello Vélez, Ildefonso
1969   *Historia de Coahuila.* Saltillo: Escuela Normal de Coahuila.

Wallerstein, Immanuel I.
1979   *The Capitalist World Economy.* Cambridge: Cambridge University Press.
1980   *The Modern World-System II, Mercantilism and the Consolidation of the European World-Economy, 1600–1750.* New York: Academic Press.

Weiss, Steven J., and Edwin C. Gooding
1968   "Estimation of Differential Employment Multipliers in a Small Regional Economy." *Land Economics* 48: 329–37.

West, Robert C., and John P. Augelli
1989   *Middle America: Its Lands and Peoples.* Englewood Cliffs, N.J.: Prentice Hall.

Whetten, Nathan L.
1948   *Rural Mexico.* Chicago: University of Chicago Press.

Wiest, Raymond E.
1979   "Implications of International Labor Migration for Mexican Rural Development." In Fernando Camara and Robert Van Kemper, eds., *Migration Across Frontiers: Mexico and the United States.* Albany: Institute for Mesoamerican Studies, State University of New York, pp. 85–97.
1984   "External Dependency and the Perpetuation of Temporary Migration to the United States." In Richard C. Jones, ed., *Patterns of Undocumented Migration: Mexico and the United States.* Totowa, N.J.: Rowman and Allanheld, pp. 110–35.

Zacatecas: Cuaderno de Información para la Planeación.
1986   Mexico, D.F.: INEGI (Instituto Nacional de Estadística Geografía e Informática).

Zazueta, Cesar, and Rodolfo Corona
1979   *Los Trabajadores Mexicanos en los Estados Unidos: Primeros Resultados de la Encuesta Nacional de Emigración a la Frontera Norte del País y a los Estados Unidos.* México, D.F.: Centro Nacional de Información y Estadísticos del Trabajo (CENIET).

Index

About the Author

Richard C. Jones has been studying Mexican migration to the United States for the past fifteen years and has published some twenty articles on the topic in journals such as *International Migration Review, The Annals of the Association of American Geographers, Economic Geography, National Geographic Research, The Social Science Quarterly, The Journal of Geography,* and *The Journal of Borderland Scholars,* in addition to a previous book, *Patterns of Undocumented Migration: Mexico and the United States* (1984). His early Mexican research focused on spatial patterns of origins and destinations and their historical and demographic contexts; later research has analyzed impacts on destinations in Mexico. The receipt of a major grant from the National Science Foundation enabled the author to spend six months interviewing in Mexico (January–June 1988), collecting the data for this book. Recently, the author was awarded a Fulbright–García Robles Senior Research Scholarship to the Instituto de Geografía (UNAM) in Mexico City (January–June 1994), to study the impact of trade liberalization on emigrant regions of central Mexico. His wife, Maria Maya Jones, who is from Mexico City, has been his research assistant and companion during the past six years of intermittent study and travel in Mexico.

Richard Jones is Associate Professor of Geography in the Division of Social and Policy Sciences at the University of Texas at San Antonio.